DREW STEVEN BECKER

VISION

WHAT STARTS WITH A ?

IN

WILL END WITH A !

ACTION

YOUR BEST DAYS ARE AHEAD

ISBN-13: 978-0-578-71756-2

CONTENTS

*To My Beloved Parents who loved me
through the worst of times and the best of times.*

*I am eternally grateful for your love that you demonstrated over the years
through sacrificing your time, energy, and money for me and my family.*

Words will never express my gratitude.

INTRODUCTION

I finished writing this book before the COVID-19 pandemic broke loose throughout the Earth. Shortly after returning from Uganda, Africa on February 29, 2020, businesses and churches began to close down to flatten the curve of the virus so our healthcare workers wouldn't be overwhelmed. Life began to change quickly and so did our vocabulary: flatten the curve, social distancing, quarantine, shutdown, coronavirus, COVID-19, Wuhan Virus, reset, sanitizer, elbow bumps, Zoom, Facebook Live, online service only, reopen, and cancellations.

During the first two weeks of abrupt shutdowns and massive changes in our society, I heard the still small voice of Heaven speaking loud and clear, "Don't stop dreaming." Those three words led me through the weightiness of the pandemic season, along with many other messages of great comfort from other messengers and from God Himself.

This book is not just about dreaming, but taking steps to walk out the Heavenly dream that God has for each of us. Thus, "Vision in Action." What is a dream without action? It's simply a dream we talk about but never really discover. Sounds disappointing right? It's my prayer and desire to encourage, equip, and empower you to not only dream about the Heavenly vision, but to walk it out with God.

Take a journey with me as we observe the Biblical character, Nehemiah, start his journey with a question. You may have more questions than answers about God's plan for your life, but like Nehemiah, may what started with a question end with an exclamation!

CHAPTER 1

IT STARTS WITH A QUESTION

"And I *asked* them concerning the Jews who escaped, who had survived the exile, and concerning Jerusalem."

(Nehemiah 1:2b)

"Our lives are shaped by the questions we ask. Good questions lead to good outcomes. Bad questions lead to bad outcomes."

(Michael Hyatt)

Twenty-eight years ago, I asked a dangerous question, "God, what do you want me to do in this world?" I was standing and praying in an efficiency apartment one evening in Fargo, ND, when I asked this life-changing question. The apartment building was located on Elm Street. Yes, my life at the time was like a "Nightmare on Elm Street," at least that's what it felt like. I was twenty-two years old, depressed, and had no clue what I was going to do with my life. Catch my drift?

After several months of struggling with thoughts of suicide and severe depression, I was beyond desperate. I was receiving godly counsel, taking my vitamin B12 pills, rebuking every devil known to mankind, confessing God's promises, and declaring my new Identity in Christ. All that was good, but I still didn't know what I was specifically created for. I've felt the call of God to preach since I was fifteen, but wondered how that was going to happen when I could barely get my head off the pillow every morning.

I did something that night which changed my life forever—I asked a question. I asked the right question. "God, what do *You* want me to do in this world?" Michael W. Smith's song, "Place In This World" was released just months before I asked this big question. I found myself on many occasions singing along with Michael:

> Looking for a reason
> Roaming through the night to find
> My place in this world
> My place in this world
> Not a lot to lean on
> I need Your light to help me find
> My place in this world
> My place in this world[1]

No, I wasn't waving a Bic lighter or my phone's flashlight (of course, cell phones back then were bag phones), I was singing along with Michael and tears would often stream down my face as I was crying out for "My place in this world." On this fall night in 1991, the cry of my heart got answered by Heaven.

Sometimes the hardest activity under Heaven is simply listening. After asking, "God, what do *You* want me to do in this world?" What I heard in my heart was, "Lay your hands on the maps of North and South Dakota." I was a map freak in college. I loved maps. So, I did what I heard. I believed the still small voice (1 Kings 19:12, KJV) and laid my hands on the maps of the Dakotas.

When I put my hands on the maps, I began to see with the eyes of my heart (Ephesians 1:18) flames of fire popping up in the small towns of the Dakotas. I began to see and hear God's heart for these small towns. He wanted Kingdom-minded churches impacting them. He wanted passionate, Holy Spirit-filled churches to be established for His purposes on the Earth, and somehow and some way, I knew He wanted me to be a part of this plan.

Nehemiah's call began with a question, "And I asked them concerning the Jews who escaped, who had survived the exile, and concerning Jerusalem" (Nehemiah 1:2b). God's purpose and plan for our lives often begins with a question. Nehemiah was interested in the condition of his people in Jerusalem. His question started a dialogue that would eventually disturb him enough to disrupt any of his plans to remain comfortable in the palace. The answer from his brother and friends was, "The remnant there in the province who had survived the exile is in great trouble and shame. The wall of Jerusalem is broken down, and its gates are destroyed by fire" (Nehemiah 1:3). The answer to Nehemiah's question wasn't what he wanted to hear, but it's what he needed to hear.

Nehemiah's question led to an answer which initiated a stirring in his heart. Pay attention to the questions of your heart. Within the question lies dormant the answer. Sometimes the answer isn't what you want to hear, but it's the very thing that fires up your passion toward your purpose for existence. My heart's cry became my call. To this day, I enjoy helping people walk in their God-given destiny, and remain passionate to see churches planted in small towns. One question will lead to another. For me it started with, "What is my place in this world?" to, "Are there any Gospel-preaching churches in this town?" then, "How can I raise up leaders to pastor churches in these small towns?" One question leads to another. Your destiny is found in the question of your heart. Don't negate the question of your heart.

Nehemiah's question catapulted him into his destiny. He was a cupbearer for the king. He was a high-ranking official in the king's palace who was entrusted to protect the king from poisoning.[2] Though his position may have been risky at times, Nehemiah was living in the palace. He was in a comfortable place. God has a way of making the comfortable, uncomfortable. He delights in stirring His People out of the nest of convenience and complacency. How does He do it? He does it by placing inside of us, a question. The question may come from something that frustrates you. For example:

Why do they do what they do?
Does anyone else see the need here?
Why isn't anyone reaching out to them?
Why am I so unsatisfied with my job?
How can this be accomplished more efficiently?
How can this be done better?
Why am I so frustrated?

Where is my passion?

Questions can reveal change. I was a Youth Pastor from 1994-2000 in Beulah, ND. I loved what I was doing. I had no lack of passion or energy for that calling and position. In 1999, I began to become restless. I had questions. "Why am I not as passionate as I was before? Why is Twyla weeping over the condition of these youths and I'm not?" Twyla Kuntz had been one of the youth kids when I first started. She graduated and then went to Trinity Bible College to be trained in ministry. Before her final year of college, she interned under Christi and I in the summer of 1999. She's the only person I know who successfully locked themselves in the bathroom and couldn't get out. I should have known then that she had some unique gifts for youth ministry.

During Twyla's Christmas break in 1999, she came home from college. During that break, she helped us in the Youth Ministry. After one of the Wednesday night services, everyone left except Twyla. She stayed to pray over our youth. She was weeping for our youth. That night I knew my time was done. I had already been wrestling with questions and receiving confirmations to travel full time in ministry. But when I saw this passion rising within Twyla, I knew it was time for me to pass the baton.

This wasn't easy for Christi and I. We loved these youths and deeply enjoyed our ministry with Pastors Ron and Julie Enget. It was a pleasure of ours to be part of a great ministry team. Plus, I had just received a very nice raise. This was a pull for me to stay because our first child, Nehemiah, was about to be born. This stirring didn't seem logical nor did it appear affordable. Questions began to arise within me, questions such as, "How will I get meetings? What will I say? How do I get started? How will I get paid? What in the world am I doing?" At times, I felt like I had more questions than answers. But the bottom line was this: the passion to preach from town to town was greater than the passion to be a Youth Pastor. I couldn't get the small towns off of my mind.

We all need good friends and mentors in our life who will tell us what we need to hear. Dean Niforatos has been that person in my life many times. Dean came to Beulah in December of 1999 to preach at our New Year's event for our youth. After about one day of being with us in Beulah, Dean walked into my office and said abruptly and with much conviction, "Dude, your time is done in Beulah." Can you get any more direct than that? The only thing I could say was, "I know." Then I asked, "Will you please tell Pastors Ron and Julie for me?" Seems like a cop out right? Actually, I had attempted to talk to them about what I was feeling, but that conversation never seemed to take flight. Dean responded with an absolute "YES!" Later that day, he met with Pastors Ron and Julie and dropped the bomb.

I thank God for friends who see the future with you. I thank God for leaders who walk with you during seasons of transition. Dean saw the future and was bold enough to declare it and share it. Pastors Ron and Julie were gracious enough to walk with us through it. Sometimes, when leaders know you are transitioning out of their network, they become offended and cut the friendship off, but not Ron & Julie. They did the opposite. They assisted us, blessed us, and launched us out to the next phase of our ministry.

Someone once said, "The first step to receiving an answer is being brave enough to ask a question" (Anonymous). I sometimes wonder if Nehemiah had a hunch about the condition of the Jews in Jerusalem. I imagine the question of his heart was ruminating within him before he asked the big question. I'm sure that happens to you. You know something intuitively, but you're too afraid to ask. What's the question of your heart? What's stirring inside of you today? It's time to ask. It's time to move forward with God's plan for your life. Can you hear Him calling?

Action Steps

1. Invest in a Dream Journal.
2. What are the burning questions of your heart? Write them down in your new journal.
3. Allow yourself to dream and follow the flow when you write.
4. Meditate and Journal your thoughts on the following Scripture: "Where there is no vision, the people perish: but he that keepeth the law, happy is he" (Proverbs 29:18, KJV).

Notes

1. Michael W. Smith, Amy Grant and Wayne Kirkpatrick, "Place In This World," 1990, track 3 on *Go West Young Man*, Reunion, 1991, compact disc.
2. *Encyclopaedia Judaica*. (Jerusalem: Encyclopaedia Judaica, 1996).

CHAPTER 2

THE ART OF LISTENING

"As soon as I heard these words, I sat down and wept and mourned for days, and I continued fasting and praying before the God of heaven."

(Nehemiah 1:4)

"The word 'listen' contains the same letters as the word 'silent.'"

(Alfred Brendel)

We have been created with two ears and one mouth for a reason. I would like to believe I listen more than I talk, but that might not be the case. My daughter, Mercy, said, "Everyone in this family talks so much." I had to laugh. Maybe it has something to do with my wife, Christi, and I both being pastors? I like to preach and Christi loves greeting people every Sunday morning at Freedom Church. Most Sundays, we're the last ones out the door. My kids love that.

Listening to God and listening to others is serious business. We can make a ton of mistakes by simply not listening. When you have a personality like mine, listening doesn't come naturally. Dean Jackson says, "Listening is an art that requires attention over talent, spirit over ego, others over self." Why do I think I have the answer before I have heard the question in full? You know what I mean? Christi is a patient person, thank God! But, when I decide to fill in the blank with my "wise" answers without hearing the question in full, I'm not so wise.

Stephen Covey says, "Most people do not listen with the intent to understand; they listen with the intent to reply." Understanding comes with listening. Christi and I have been married for twenty-two years. I've discovered why she knows more about people than I do. She listens to understand. We can be sitting in the same conversation with other people, and she often has more information and understanding from that conversation than me. Why? I'm trying to fix the problem before I understand their circumstances and hear their hearts speaking.

I've discovered, "Listening is often the only thing needed to help someone" (Anonymous). Most people discover the answer to their dilemma after they have been able to "talk it out" with someone. Because of my discovery years ago, I've learned a few disciplines over the years to assist me in listening better:

1. I say, "Let me repeat what I believe I heard you say."
2. I write down notes of our conversation.
3. I ask questions to make sure I'm fully understanding.
4. I purposely tell myself at times, "Silence is not bad."

You may be chuckling right now. But for guys like me, I've had to learn some disciplines for the sake of building better relationships and following God's lead for my life. There's nothing worse than sharing your thoughts, struggles, and heart with someone, and feeling like something other than your conversation is swirling around in their mind. Bryan H. McGill says, "One of the most sincere forms of respect is actually listening to what another has to say." Listening = respect. When we listen, we honor God and people.

Nehemiah listened. He asked a question, and with much awareness, heard, "The remnant there in the province who had survived the exile is in great trouble and shame. The wall of Jerusalem is broken down, and its gates are destroyed by fire" (Nehemiah 1:3). This wasn't the answer he wanted to hear. It was an answer that disturbed him to the point of great sorrow.

We live in a world of chaos. Like never before, this chaos is reported right before our eyes to see and our ears to hear. It has become the norm to hear and see shootings, natural disasters, and wars all around the world. We've almost become numb to it. Nehemiah could've said, "I'm sorry to hear that. I'll pray for you and our fellow Jews in Jerusalem." He could've simply put it on his prayer list and went about business as usual, but that wasn't his reaction. Nehemiah said, "When I heard these things, I sat down and wept. For some days I mourned and fasted and prayed before the God of heaven" (Nehemiah 1:4). The question invited an answer, and the answer demanded a response—one that would change Nehemiah forever.

Nehemiah heard with his physical ears and was moved with sorrow and compassion. Have you ever been moved with compassion? It's not something you'll ever forget. Several years ago, I assisted my father-in-law with shingling the roof of his garage. About five to six other guys joined us on that September morning. One of the guys was a guy named Norman. Norman wasn't on my father-in-law's "top ten list for greatest guys," if you know what I mean. He was the drug addict, Harley riding, and free-spirited guy who got my father-in-law's daughter pregnant. Not a recipe for a future son-in-law.

It was on this day in September that all of us (family) were going to meet Norman for the first time. On a roof. With about eight guys. You get the picture? I wasn't sure if my father-in-law would use the roof to his advantage, or better yet, the nail gun. There was some concern. But on that beautiful day, when Norman finally got up on the roof, I greeted him with a handshake and a "Hi, my name is Drew." What happened next totally caught me off guard. I turned around and began to weep. Yes, weep! I was on a roof shingling with seven other men. Not what I expected. I WAS MOVED WITH COMPASSION! I began to weep over the condition of Norman's soul and his eternal destiny.

Here's my point: listen to what others are saying and be attuned to the language of love. It's one thing hearing with our physical ears, but it's another hearing the cry of God's heart. You know what God's heart is? His heart is for people. God is love (1 John 4:8). When you're moved with compassion for someone, it's God's heart touching yours. He is showing you His mission. As strange and bizarre as it was that day on a roof weeping, I was stirred to pray for Norman with much passion and determination. I knew the Scripture, "The Lord is not slow to fulfill his promise as some count slowness, but is patient toward you, not wishing that any should perish, but that all should reach repentance" (2 Peter 3:9). My mission was to P.U.S.H.—Pray Until Something Happens.

After three months of praying fervently, I watched my prayers of faith move mountains. My wife directed a Christmas play at our church in Beulah, ND, and I preached a short gospel message of salvation after the play. I challenged everyone who hadn't surrendered their life to Christ to do it that day. Norman was there that Sunday. He was videotaping the play. Do you remember the old VHS tapes? Norman put down the large video camera (it was still recording), and came to the front of the church to repent and ask Christ to forgive, cleanse, and transform his life. It was the start of a new beginning for Norman and an eternal lesson for me: God moves your heart for the mission. If the mission doesn't involve people, it's probably not a Heavenly vision.

Three months after the play, a man came to visit me at my office. I didn't recognize him. It took me a while, but when he got closer to me, I finally figured it out. It was Norman. I hadn't seen him for about a month because he was working out of town. He was clean-shaven and had cut his long hair. Don't get me wrong, I don't think you need to be clean-shaven or have your hair short and parted on the side to be a stellar Christian. But for Norman, it was a statement: "God has touched my heart and I'm celebrating the change of heart with my change of looks." We had a good conversation that day, but it would be our last conversation on this planet.

In February of that year, Norman's heart went into complete shock and he died within a few short minutes. He was with his friends and my sister-in-law when his heart exploded. Christi and I got a phone call and we hurried to the hospital. We followed the ambulance to the hospital in Hazen, ND. We prayed, we waited to hear, and then we cried. Tears still come to my eyes as I'm writing. We were numb with shock but comforted by this fact: I was moved with compassion. We prayed, we believed, we saw God save a man from the guttermost, and now, he's with Jesus in the uttermost!

It's important that we listen with our natural ears and our spiritual ears. Nehemiah listened to his brethren and God's love that moved him with compassion. God's vision will move you to action, if you listen. Nehemiah prayed, fasted, and made a plan to journey to Jerusalem. His life would change forever. Are you prepared to listen? Are you ready for movement? That's what Vision in Action is about. It's more than a "Dreamer's Dream" that's never experienced. It's about the question of your heart, the answer from Heaven, and the listening ears that hear the cry of people and the call of Heaven.

Action Steps

1. Ask three friends and/or family members, "Do I listen well?"
2. Listen to their answers and journal them.
3. Find a peaceful place. Ask God the questions of your heart. Listen and write the answers in your journal. Remember, follow the flow.
4. Be aware of subtle promptings, dreams, or pictures you see in your mind's eye. Write them down.
5. Meditate and Journal your thoughts on the following Scripture: "My dearest brothers and sisters, take this to heart: Be quick to listen, but slow to speak. And be slow to become angry" (James 1:19, TPT).

CHAPTER 3

THE POWER OF PRAYER
AND FASTING

"I continued fasting and praying before the God of heaven."

(Nehemiah 1:4b)

"Fasting is found throughout the Bible. It always seems to show up when ordinary men need extraordinary power, provision, and perseverance to overcome impossible odds, enemies, or obstructions."

(Mahesh Chavda)

Action without prayer is dangerous. Action after a time of prayer and fasting can be revolutionary. If you've ever felt stuck or at a standstill with your God-given vision, prayer and fasting will position you for a breakthrough. Sometimes the water gets stagnant and we need the flow back in our lives. I found prayer and fasting effective in loosening the blockages, permitting the flow of vision in our lives. Prayer and fasting doesn't change God's perspective, it reforms ours. Sometimes we simply need the pipe to be aligned, so the water can flow again. Prayer and fasting are about us becoming aligned with God's heart and the season He wants us to enter.

Nehemiah said, "I continued fasting and praying." Nehemiah was not only moved with compassion, but was stirred to take action. He was desperate. There's nothing wrong with taking action through prayer and fasting in seasons of desperation. Prayer and fasting are a declaration of surrender. We're literally saying, "God, I need you! I cannot move forward without your direction in my life!" Along with being stirred to take action, Nehemiah felt the remorse of his sin and his people's backsliding. He was immediately awakened to his need for alignment with God's plans and purposes. He cried out in prayer, "Let your ear be attentive and your eyes open, to hear the prayer of your servant that I now pray before you day and night for the people of Israel your servants, confessing the sins of the people of Israel, which we have sinned against you. Even I and my father's house have sinned" (Nehemiah 1:6). This is a picture of getting the pipes cleaned out.

Most of the books I've read on vision don't discuss the importance of repentance. Nehemiah was repenting for his sins and the sins of his people. The Apostle Paul wrote, "Godly sorrow brings repentance that leads to salvation and leaves no regret, but worldly sorrow brings death" (2 Corinthians 7:10). The sorrow Nehemiah felt led him to repentance. Repentance is a good thing. The Greek word for repent is "metanoeō." It means, "To think differently,[1] the change of mind of those who have begun to abhor their errors and misdeeds, and have determined to enter upon a better course of life, so that it embraces both a recognition of sin and sorrow for it and hearty amendment, the tokens and effects of which are good deeds."[2] Nehemiah was literally embracing God's vision for his life through Godly sorrow, repentance, prayer, and fasting.

I've learned a few things about prayer and fasting through the years, mostly good, some bad. The first time I fasted, I was trying to change God's mind. That didn't work. I felt God leading me out of a relationship, but I didn't want to let go. I thought this girl was the one, but I knew God had a different opinion. I decided to borrow a friend's tent so I could get away from food and other distractions. I pitched my tent out at Richmond Lake near my hometown, Aberdeen, SD. I began to pray and fast. My quest was to find the will of God, although I already knew it. I was attempting to change God's plan. My goal was to pray and fast a few days and see what would happen. It lasted about three hours. I drove to the Lake's resort, ate a hotdog, and talked to someone about Jesus. God always wins! That's an example of a bad fasting.

Good fasting is when you have a clear objective and a surrendered heart. In 1994, the church I was interning with called for a regional time of prayer and fasting. Pastors from the region joined us in this time of calling out to God and believing for an Awakening in our Nation. I was specifically praying and fasting for an open door to minister full-time. Toward the end of that time of prayer and fasting, I met Ron Enget from Beulah, ND. He introduced himself and asked, "How would you like to come to Beulah, ND, and become my Youth Pastor?" I said, "Yes. I would like that." He had a funny look on his face as if he was thinking, "How in the world can you say 'yes' so quick?" It was simple. I was praying and fasting and I was desperate. I had no other options or invites. I quickly felt this was an answer from God! I spent nine years of my life in Beulah, ND. Prayer and fasting aligns us to the will of God for our lives. It opens doors that no man can shut!

In 2002, I heard in my spirit, "I want you to pray and fast twenty-one days, three separate times this year." I didn't necessarily like hearing that. I thought, "God, is that really you?" It was. Please don't think that prayer and fasting is the answer to all of your woes. I'm certainly not saying this is the only way to get breakthroughs or hear clearly from God. As a word to the wise, prayer and fasting is an act of your will, but God will certainly lead you to set aside special times for prayer and fasting. Also, if you've never fasted and prayed, please become informed of all the physical aspects of fasting. You have to be well equipped and prepared to fast in a healthy way.

Each of those fasts in 2002 changed my life and the people closest to me. After one of the twenty-one-day fasts, I experienced the Hand of God move in a way I'll never forget. I had just returned home to Beulah from a series of meetings I had preached in another town. Christi was pregnant with our second child, Ezekiel Isaac. She was about to pop. Every part of her was swollen and at any time she could deliver. We traveled to Bismarck to get a final ultrasound to see how the baby was doing. The Doctor said, "This baby is big and positioned upside down in the womb. Your baby needs to turn before he births or this will be more difficult." Not exactly the words you want to hear.

That weekend in Beulah, our church was hosting meetings with Bobby Conner. Bobby is a gifted man. He flows in the revelatory gifts of God: prophecy, words of knowledge, words of wisdom, and discernment (1 Cor. 12:1-8). It was the last day of the conference in the afternoon when Christi and I went to the front of the church for prayer. Bobby gently asked, "Can I pray for your wife and over her womb?" I said, "Sure." Bobby asked me to put my hand on Christi's belly (it was sticking out to Texas) and then he said he would put his hand on my hand. The first thing he said after laying his hand on mine was, "I see this child is positioned in the wrong direction." We were shocked! We said, "You are seeing right." Then Bobby moved his hand and said, "The Hand of God is moving this child in the right direction." Sounds crazy, right?

Christi felt warmth and then felt nauseous. She had to walk briskly to the bathroom because she thought she was going to vomit. Our Pastor and Worship Leader were watching the whole thing as Bobby was praying. They both said, "I saw Christi's shirt move as the baby moved." I thought, this is crazy! But I liked it! On Monday, we went back to Bismarck. Normally, the Doctor doesn't order an ultrasound right before delivery, but in our case, he wanted to see the baby's position so he knew how to prepare. This is what we heard from the nurse, "Your baby has turned! This is good." I said, "You want to know how?" I told her the whole story. I'm not sure she believed a word I was saying.

What most people didn't know about this story at the time was that I had just finished a twenty-one day fast. When we found out Ezekiel had moved to the right position, I heard in my spirit, "Now your ministry is headed in the right direction." I had many interpretations of that immediately. The first question I should've asked was, "God, what do you mean by this?" Instead, I interpreted it to mean we would have more meetings, increase of income, and many more breakthroughs. Well, those things happened, but ultimately it meant a geographical move back to my hometown, Aberdeen. One year later, we moved, and we've been living in "The Hub City" ever since. Prayer and fasting brings you into alignment with your assignment.

Nehemiah was coming into alignment with his assignment. God created him to be a revivalist, reformer, and mighty leader for his people. At the time, he was a cupbearer for the king. This was his assignment for a season, but now he was being aligned for the next. Nehemiah had to repent. He had to begin seeing what God was saying over him. He did that through prayer, fasting, and repentance. His spiritual eyes were becoming awakened for a new day—one that would change the course of his life and impact a Nation for God's Glory.

After our family moved to Aberdeen, I began to ask the same question day after day, week after week, and month after month: "Why did we move here?" Once again, I had my own interpretation and it didn't include becoming a pastor. A few of my pastor friends thought we moved to Aberdeen to start a church. I fought that in my head. I thought to myself, "Start a church in my hometown? I'm not sure that will work. I don't want to stop traveling." I would then put it out of my mind and not even consider their thoughts or the gentle prophetic rumblings. When you struggle with the same gnawing thought for months, you have to come to peace. So, I decided to pray and fast for twenty-eight days. Why twenty-eight days? I can't remember why. But I knew I would end the fast a few days before my thirty-fifth birthday. Remember, prayer and fasting aligns your heart and will with the will of God. Fasting is a choice to humble yourself before God. I was seeking direction. I was wanting to answer the question of my heart and mind: "Why did we move to Aberdeen?" Around the fifteenth day of my fast, I heard and saw something that would change my life forever. I went from resistance to acceptance. My mind went from partly cloudy to clear blue skies. I was being aligned and set on course for my next assignment.

I heard, "Hub inside The Hub," and then I saw a Hub in a wheel with spokes projecting out from the Hub. I knew what it meant. My spirit was alert. I knew we were being called to start a church in Aberdeen and multiple other churches would be planted from the Hub. I began to hear and see what I was called to do for the next several years of my life. I was coming into alignment with Heaven's assignment. The fog began to clear.

At the end of the twenty-eight day fast, I met Christi and the boys in Beulah. I was coming back from a ministry trip and my family decided to spend a few days back in Beulah with Christi's family. The church was hosting meetings with a "fireball" by the name of Julaine Christensen. Julaine began ministering to people at the altar toward the end of the meeting that night. She was gently speaking over people until she got to me. She laid hands on my head and began to declare with much force and fire, "You have a decision to make! You have a radical decision to make! You are a radical!" I can't remember all the words she spoke over me that night, but I know this for sure, that her words confirmed the call. Prayer and fasting not only aligns you, but prepares you for the words of confirmation you need to receive. Prayer and fasting are a posture of desperation that pulls on the prophetic anointing.

That twenty-eight day fast changed my life forever. Now Christi wasn't quite in agreement with our new assignment. She was apprehensive and not sure this was God's plan for us. But, six months later, Christi fasted and prayed for twenty-one days to hear from Heaven and erase any doubts she may have about our new assignment. Toward the end of her fast, we were ministering in Beulah, ND. After I got done speaking and ministering to people that night, Jeff Kopp stood behind the mic and said, "Drew and Christi, I know you are living in Aberdeen and it's called 'The Hub City,' but what I hear is, 'Drew and Christi, you are the Hub.'" What didn't make sense to him made sense to me. I turned to Christi and said, "I told you." God was calling us to be "the Hub inside The Hub" and it was being confirmed to Christi and solidified in my mind and spirit.

Prayer and fasting brings you into a place of surrender. We become dulled by the world around us and lulled by the fantasies of comfort before us. I was becoming comfortable with traveling full-time. I could, like other evangelists, have said, "Blow in, blow up, and then blow out." It's easier to stir the masses than to help steer them. Nehemiah was probably becoming comfortable in the palace. It was only for a season. We often attempt to put down our stakes when God is wanting us to put up our sails. Nehemiah was stirred to pray and fast so he could come into alignment with his new assignment. He was being prepared to launch out from the shore and into the depths of God's great vision for his life.

Are you feeling stuck? Maybe it's time to pray and fast? The calling on your life is too great to forfeit. The clouds are about to be removed by the winds of change. Your daily dose of confusion can be replaced with a delightful meal of peace that comes when you surrender to God in prayer and fasting. God is for you! He wants to show you His plan for your life. Don't wait! Don't hesitate!

Get informed and prepare yourself for action! The vision is real. It will not tarry forever.

Action Steps

1. Choose one day to pray and fast. Don't put it off. Mark it down on your calendar today and do it within the next ten days.
2. Carve out time on that day to pray, listen, and write.
3. Ask someone to pray and fast with you. Ask them to pray over your life and the vision God wants you to walk in. Ask them to journal any thoughts they get. Tell your friend or family member, "I will return the favor."
4. Meditate and Journal your thoughts on the following Scripture: "But when you pray, go into your room and shut the door and pray to your Father who is in secret. And your Father who sees in secret will reward you" (Matthew 6:6).

Notes

1. Strong's Hebrew Lexicon (KJV), Blue Letter Bible, accessed November 7, 2019, www.blueletterbible.org, G3340.
2. Thayer's Greek Lexicon Electronic Database, copyright © 2002, 2003, 2006, 2011 by Biblesoft, Inc., accessed November 5, 2019, www.blueletterbible.org.

CHAPTER 4

REPENT AND SEE

"Let your ear be attentive and your eyes open, to hear the prayer of your servant that I now pray before you day and night for the people of Israel your servants, confessing the sins of the people of Israel, which we have sinned against you. Even I and my father's house have sinned."

(Nehemiah 1:6)

"To repent is to adopt God's viewpoint in place of your own."

(William Temple)

Fasting humbles your soul to see as God sees. Repentance is seeing what God sees, and then choosing to follow His heart and purpose for your life. Some people view the word "repent" as something distasteful or offensive, but the word is hopeful and life-giving if completely understood. The word "repent" means to turn or change one's mind. Jesus' message was, "Repent, for the Kingdom of God is at hand." He didn't have his finger pointing, his mouth quivering, and his eyes squinting as He said it. Jesus was declaring to the masses, "I am now here, everything is going to be different. The new covenant is being established through me. Watch the Kingdom in action as I heal the sick, raise the dead, and cast out demons." In order for us to grab hold of the new, we have to let go of the old. Old mindsets must change. We must see as He sees and do as He does.

"Repentance, as we know, is basically not moaning and remorse, but turning and change" (J.I. Packer). Nehemiah was moaning and groaning, but his remorse led to true repentance, which is a change of mind and action. Growing up with an older sister was great! My sister, Kendra, is an absolute gem. But while we were growing up, I loved to pick on her. I was ruthless at times. When I was about eighteen or nineteen, I knew I had gone too far in the goading, so I apologized and said to Kendra, "I'm sorry." Her response was a game changer for me. She said, "No you're not. If you were sorry, you would stop." Ouch! OUCH! The truth hurts, right? I pondered her reply for days. I decided after that day to stop badgering my sister. Feeling remorse may be the start of repentance, but it definitely isn't complete without change. Steven J. Lawson says, "If your repentance has not changed your life, you need to repent of your repentance." True repentance is more than a feeling and a confession, it's a change of direction.

Nehemiah was deeply grieved about the condition of the walls in Jerusalem. Over a period of four months, he was sorrowful over his sins and the sins of his forefathers. He began to make an important connection. The connection was this: the walls down are in direct correlation to our lack of obedience and rebellion to the plans of God. His sorrow turned into a realization. His new revelation transpired into a confession, and his sorrow and confession developed into action. Bottom line, repentance is changing one's course. It's not enough to cry, complain, and moan. It's not enough to simply confess to assuage your own conscience. Change is the fruit of true repentance, and real fruit will manifest when you truly repent.

Nehemiah made confession for the sins of Israel and he confessed on behalf of his father and himself. Sounds like a revival! Sounds like an awakening! Nehemiah identified with the sins of his forefathers. He was truly sorrowful for his Nation's backsliding. He could've pointed his finger at those who went before him and said, "Because of you rebels, me and my generation are in this place." He could've played the victim card and settled for defeat. True confession of sin realizes and identifies, it doesn't blame. I've said it a thousand times over the years, "Revival begins with me!" True change will never develop until I'm enveloped with the revelation of my responsibility.

Nehemiah didn't flippantly make a confession. His confession was from a revelation of what he and his people had done to offend God. When asking for forgiveness from someone, don't be evasive. Be clear. Communicate what you've done to offend the person, and just as important, communicate why. If you can communicate "the what," then the person knows you realize what you've done is offensive. To answer "the why," you show the personal awareness of your motivation. True repentance is going to the root. I'm not sure who first coined the phrase, "Trace the fruit to the root," but I've heard it said and have said it for years. Nehemiah goes to the root of their sin when he prays, "We have acted very corruptly against you and have not kept the commandments, the statutes, and the rules that you commanded your servant Moses. Remember the word that you commanded your servant Moses, saying, 'If you are unfaithful, I will scatter you among the peoples'" (Nehemiah 1:7-8). What was the fruit? Acting corruptly. What was the root? Rebellion.

Saint John Chrysostom said, "Be ashamed when you sin, not when you repent." Nehemiah was ashamed, but he repented. He turned from rebellion to God's perfect plan. Conviction is good for the soul, but condemnation is not a meal you want to eat every day for the rest of your life. When you turn from your sin and walk in God's plan for your life, I have good news today. You've been forgiven and God sets up a highway of restoration for you to walk on. Tony Evans says, "When you repent and operate on God's standards, now you have restoration and reconciliation." Stop trying to pay for your sins and lost time. Make the most of today! Talk with God and walk with God. He will lead, restore, and get you on the path you are to walk on. Condemnation never heals nor gives one hope. Conviction brings an awakening to your soul. You come alive to the reality of your sins and the acute awareness of God's love and plan for your life. Nehemiah was sorrowful, he made confession, and then he began to see the purpose of his present position as the cupbearer for the king. God is our redeemer.

Action Steps

1. Ask God, "Is there anything blocking my view of You and Your vision for my life?"

2. Write in your journal the thoughts you are receiving. Remember, God's heart is not to condemn you, but to encourage you. He will discipline His Children, but that discipline comes with faith, hope, and love.

3. Ask yourself, "What steps can I make to change?" Write them down and ask someone to keep you accountable. Remember, the responsibility of accountability is primarily yours. You must be honest and open with someone you trust.

4. Meditate and Journal your thoughts on the following Scripture: "Therefore, confess your sins to one another and pray for one another, that you may be healed. The prayer of a righteous person has great power as it is working" (James 5:16).

CHAPTER 5

THE RIGHT PERSON.
THE RIGHT PLACE.
THE RIGHT TIME.

"Now I was cupbearer to the king."

(Nehemiah 1:11b)

"It's not enough to be in the right place at the right time. You have to be the right person in the right place at the right time."

(T. Harv Eker)

Have you ever asked, "What am I doing here? Why here? Why now?" I'm sure Nehemiah had those questions. He was born a captive in a foreign land. His generation was heavily impacted by the sins of their forefathers. Because of sin and rebellion, God allowed His own people to go into seventy years of Babylonian captivity. The Prophet Jeremiah said to these rebellious people, "When seventy years are completed for Babylon, I will visit you, and I will fulfill to you my promise and bring you back to this place. For I know the plans I have for you, declares the Lord, plans for welfare and not for evil, to give you a future and a hope" (Jeremiah 29:10-11). The prophetic promise was true, and thousands of God's people went back to Jerusalem seventy years later to lay the foundation for the new Temple. God is our redeemer!

Nehemiah was not one of the persons "whose spirit God had stirred" (Ezra 1:5) to go on the first expedition back to Jerusalem. In fact, Nehemiah wasn't even born. His calling came over one hundred years after the first captives had returned to Jerusalem. Though the Temple had been constructed, it wasn't completed until the walls around it were erected by Nehemiah and his proficient team of builders. God doesn't start things without finishing them. Our finite minds sometimes can't comprehend God's grand plan and the people He anoints to work with Him on that plan. He has a generational perspective. One generation builds upon the floor of another. We're in this together! Nehemiah didn't know many of the good people who laid the foundation of the Temple, but he was connected to them through God's plan and purpose.

I didn't know my grandfather, Floyd E. Becker, but I know his story and I'm keenly aware it's connected to me. My grandfather was one of the first "gang-bangers" of South Dakota (that's not the connection). He was a drive-by shooter on the plains of the Dakotas. He rode bareback on a horse with a gun. Him and his cronies would ride their horses while shooting out windows. Needless to say, he found himself in trouble. But God had a plan. Remember, God is our redeemer! He takes a mess and makes a message out of it. My grandfather found himself at a crossroads in life—choose jail or go to war. Guess what he chose? A man will often choose the battle over the brig. He went to war.

What do you think Floyd did in World War I? He was a messenger. He delivered messages from the back lines to the front lines, and the front lines to the rear. His mode of transportation was, you guessed it, a horse. I'm kicking into a Keith Green song right now, "There is a Redeemer, Jesus, God's own son..." Wow! God will use your messy past to prepare you for present assignments. He sees the beginning from the end. My grandfather was in the line of fire but God knew what He was doing. He took a five-foot-two rebellious kid and put him on a horse, where eventually he would be broken enough for God's Glory! I'm preaching now, can you feel it? Floyd was under fire, but the fire of God would eventually consume him and his past sins.

My grandfather cried out to God when he was in Germany, "If you get me out of here alive, I will serve you the rest of my life!" God never forgets our prayers. Many times, I've cried out to God, "Why am I going through this fiery trial?"

He's faithful to remind me of the times I lay at the altar of First Assembly of God in Fargo, ND, crying out to God, "I'll do whatever you want me to do! Change me, God, into your image!" We forget our cry when we're in the fire, but God is faithful to answer and produce inside of us a holy resolve to finish strong.

Floyd E. Becker came back from the war without injury. God preserved him. Did he remember his vow? Not immediately, but eventually. One night, Floyd and his wife, Martha, went to a tent revival meeting in Lebanon, South Dakota. The fiery Pentecostal preacher called people to repentance and salvation. Floyd said to Martha, "Let's go. It's time to get out of here." My dad and Uncle Gene told me the story. Floyd and Martha were driving down the old gravel road outside of Lebanon when they both saw a fireball come shooting down from the sky and onto the road in front of them. Then the fireball appeared to be coming down the road after them. At that moment, Floyd turned the car around, drove back to the tent, and bowed his knees at the altar of God's cleansing fire. God is our Redeemer! He's our Reminder too! My grandpa went from firing bullets, to bullets firing at him, then surrendering to the One True Fire, "For our God is a consuming fire" (Hebrews 12:29). His fire cleanses, purifies, and makes whole.

From that experience, Floyd and Martha served Jesus. Grandpa Floyd was far from perfect, but God started something in him and through him, coupled with a generational perspective. My dad grew up in church, but slowly became cold to God and church throughout his twenties and thirties. He had a form of religion, but wasn't committed through relationship with God. He was in obligation rather than revelation. But God had a plan. At the age of thirty-nine, my dad began to realize how lost he really was. Thank God for a praying mother! My grandma Martha was a prayer warrior. Her cry became my call. I'm convinced of it! She prayed often and she prayed loud. In fact, shortly after my mom and dad came to Christ, Grandma Martha went to Glory. She died Christmas day of 1979. I've never forgotten her and the sacrifices she made at the altar. Eyes filled with tears but a heart full of faith that her sons would come back to Jesus! She won! She beat the devil through her prayers and authority in Jesus Christ!

What's my point? God sees the beginning from the end. He has a generational perspective. You are here, in this hour, for a specific purpose. You are the right person, at the right place, and at the right time! He doesn't make mistakes. You may be thinking, "I've failed miserably. How could God anoint a mess like me?" Messes are His specialty. Not that He has created them, but He certainly has redeemed them. Nehemiah was born at the perfect time and place. His forefathers made a mess through their sin and rebellion, but God wasn't done. No, God had a plan and He executed that plan through the generations. He chose Nehemiah to be the one who would finish what He had started. God was faithful to preserve Nehemiah throughout his childhood and teenage years, and then promote him to a place of influence as the cupbearer.

The cupbearer, according to Derek Kidner, "...was a high official in the royal household, whose basic duty of choosing and tasting the wine to demonstrate that it was not poisoned, and of presenting it to the king, gave him frequent access to the king's presence and made him potentially a man of influence."[1] Nehemiah was at the right place at the right time, and the one who orchestrated this was none other than God Himself. God knew Nehemiah would need access to the king. In the Kingdom, everything flows out of relationship. Nehemiah not only had access to the king, he had relational equity with the king. The king learned to trust him because he faithfully served him as the cupbearer. Nehemiah was a loyal friend.

I'm not sure if Nehemiah knew why he became the cupbearer to the king. Before he was stirred by God and moved in his spirit to finish the wall, did Nehemiah have a clue what his future would look like? I believe he knew in his heart that he was created for great things, but I don't think he knew exactly what those "great things" would be nor how the "great things" would formulate and be accomplished. The peril of the prophet isn't the inability to see what God desires, it's the process by which one gets there. For linear thinkers like myself, I like straight lines and sprints. The process of God is more like a decathlon than a sprint. Sprints are simple. Point A to point B in a straight line and it's over. A decathlon is a series of ten separate events that require several different skill sets and a diversity of preparatory actions. Sign me up for the sprints! Right?

Nehemiah had a connection with his homeland through his brother and other countrymen. His brother and friends had made journeys from Susa to Jerusalem and back. They were no strangers to the homeland. They had a firm grip on the current news of Jerusalem and what could transpire without intervention. Nehemiah probably had a feeling that someday, he too, would make the journey to Jerusalem. We may call it a "bucket list" item. I'm sure it was more than just a "bucket list" item for Nehemiah. I'm confident it was a dream. A vision instilled in his spirit by God. But his question still remained, "Why am I a cupbearer to the King of Persia? Why is this taking so long? Am I just wasting my time here?" Delays don't determine our destiny, they define them.

Don't allow delay to discourage your day. The process may be painful, but it's definitely purposeful. The bottom line is: "Do you trust God?" He placed the seed (vision) in your heart, don't allow the delays to choke the growth of that tree. Dr. Myles Munroe said, "I hold a forest in my hand...in every seed there is a tree." The seed speaks of potential. The vision starts with a seed, and that seed grows when it's watered and given the proper amount of sunlight. The seed (vision) dies when it gets no water and zero sunlight. The vision needs both. About the only thing that grows in dark wet places is mold. Delays attempt to discourage and dismay. I become discouraged and dismayed when I dismiss the Heavenly vision. The Heavenly vision (seed) grows when I pray over it, speak life into it, and continue to imagine (dream) what could be. That's the water and the light. Also, surrounding myself with the right people stimulates the seed to grow. When discouragement from delays attempts to settle in my spirit, a word spoken from another can produce life or death to the seed. Surround yourself with Guardians of your galaxy. Your galaxy is the vision God has implanted inside of you. The Guardians are the ones who see the vision with you, carry the vision with you, and pray the vision with you.

Don't give up! You're the right person, at the right place, for the right time. You're in a process to become the person for God's purpose. You may see a weak seed right now, but remember, Nehemiah was the cupbearer. He was the right person, at the right place, at the right time. He was positioned for power. Influence is power. Nehemiah was influential because he was a faithful friend to the king. Be faithful with what you're doing now and to the people God has called you to serve. Don't try to push your way to the top. Be loyal, be trustworthy, and be aware...God is preparing you for the vision.

Action Steps

1. Create a timeline for your life. Draw a straight line. Above the line, write down all the positive experiences, and on the bottom, write down the negative ones. You won't remember everything, but you certainly will have highlights and lowlights that you can jot down.

2. Reminder: God restores, heals, and uses our mess and makes it a message. How have these experiences helped you to assist others in their pain?

3. Think about how each event has positively or negatively affected you. Journal your thoughts.

4. How is God using these events in your life to shape you? Have you become bitter or better?

5. Meditate and Journal your thoughts on the following Scripture: "And the God of all grace, who called you to his eternal glory in Christ, after you have suffered a little while, will himself restore you and make you strong, firm and steadfast" (1 Peter 5:10, NIV).

Notes

1. Derek Kidner, *Ezra And Nehemiah: An Introduction and Commentary*. Tyndale Old Testament Commentaries, Volume 12. General Editor: Donald J. Wiseman. (Downers Grove, IL: IVP Academic, 2009), 159.

CHAPTER 6

A TIME TO WAIT

"Early the following spring, in the month of Nisan, during the twentieth year of King Artaxerxes' reign."

(Nehemiah 2:1)

"Timing is so important! If you are going to be successful in dance, you must be able to respond to rhythm and timing. It's the same in the Spirit. People who don't understand God's timing can become spiritually spastic, trying to make the right things happen at the wrong time. They don't get His rhythm—and everyone can tell they are out of step. They birth things prematurely, threatening the very lives of their God-given dreams."

(T. D. Jakes)

Nehemiah's conversation with his brother and fellow countrymen transpired in mid-November or mid-December, 446 BC, and approximately four months later, March/April, 445, he approached the king with his request.[1] Nehemiah waited four months to communicate his vision to the king. Wisdom can be found in waiting.

I look at the waiting period as a time to become established in what God is speaking to my heart. It's a time of preparation for what's to come. My mind begins to catch up with what I'm seeing or hearing in my spirit during this season. After I heard "Hub inside The Hub" during my twenty-eight day fast, my mind had to begin receiving and believing what God was speaking to me.

It was a waiting period. A time to solidify and count the cost of what God was calling me and my family to do. I was energized by the revelation, but sober with the thought of the mission at hand. I knew this next venture of planting churches would be a calling that may continue for the entirety of my life on this planet. Thus, I waited patiently before I announced the vision to anyone.

Peter Marshall said, "Teach us, O Lord, the disciplines of patience, for to wait is often harder than to work." Waiting is not a passive activity under Heaven, at least not the waiting mentioned in the Book of Isaiah—"But they who wait for the LORD shall renew their strength; they shall mount up with wings like eagles; they shall run and not be weary; they shall walk and not faint." The Hebrew word for wait is "Qavah," pronounced "Ka-va." Its meaning is: look for, hope, expect, to look or wait eagerly for, to linger for.[2] To wait for the LORD is to be in hopeful expectation. Expectation of what? For God to speak, move or remove obstacles, and give wisdom and strength.

When you receive God's vision for your life, be quick to listen and slow to speak. Don't set a microphone to your mouth and blast it out to everyone. Be in hopeful expectation to hear further instructions from Heaven. Nehemiah was stirred to action and his first step was to listen, then wait. The waiting period for Nehemiah helped him establish four things: (1) courage to approach the king, (2) a well thought out answer for the king, (3) a strategy to carry out the vision, and (4) the conviction that he was called by God to be the leader for this mission. The key word here is *establish*. The season of waiting is a season of preparation and becoming established in your identity and strategy.

When I received the vision to start a church in Aberdeen, I waited months before I communicated the vision with anyone, other than my wife. I was waiting with a purpose. Five significant things occurred to help me become established in my time of waiting: (1) alignment and unity with my wife, (2) alignment and unity with leaders in my life, (3) confirming prophetic words, (4) development of strategy, and last and definitely not the least, (5) prayer. The truth is, difficult times will come after as you follow the Heavenly vision for your life. It's important to have unity with those closest to you, a plan, confirmations, and a solid connection to God in prayer and His Word. When these are established in your life, you'll have a reservoir of faith that you can draw from in the times of trouble. Your seasons of waiting are significant for development. What you sow in the waiting season, you will reap in the action season.

Graham Cooke talks about the process of the prophetic word. This process can be applied to the vision God has given you to fulfill. Cooke says the process looks like this: (1) REVELATION, (2) CONFRONTATION, (3) TRANS-FORMATION, and (4) MANIFESTATION. Cooke says people give up on the prophetic word in the confrontation and transformation stages. I believe the same is true with the Heavenly vision. Revelation is the energy and passion for the Purpose. It's in this stage we become awakened to the plans and purposes of God for our lives. It starts in seed form, then grows as we water it through prayer and holy imaginations. Holy imaginations are "seeing the vision" in the eyes of your spirit. You begin to imagine what could be. Another word we could use is "faith." When God spoke to Joshua, "See, I have delivered Jericho into your hands, along with its king and its fighting men" (Joshua 6:2, NIV). The walls of Jericho were still up and barricaded, "Now the gates of Jericho were securely barred because of the Israelites. No one went out and no one came in" (Joshua 6:1, NIV). When God told Joshua to "see," I believe He was inviting Joshua to see what could be by seeing through the eyes of faith. Once Joshua did, he listened to God's strategy and then took action.

Revelation gives us understanding we hadn't possessed before. What was once hidden, is now revealed. That's energizing! When you begin to see the vision of God for your life, you will be energized to fulfill God's plan. Use this God-given energy to write, ponder, and proclaim in prayer what you're seeing and believing for. When I heard that small phrase, "Hub inside The Hub," I began to dream of what could be. What I once resisted and couldn't see, was now becoming a reality in my spirit. I believe the same was true with Nehemiah. The vision began with a question, then an answer, followed by a time of crying out to God and listening to the plans God would have for him. It's like a conceiving time, then an incubation period. The baby (vision) grows in your spirit, then the birthing time comes.

I enjoy the beauty of tulips in the spring. My parents have tulips in their front and back yard. Tulips are a reminder every year that the winter is over and springtime is here. These beautiful and delicate flowers are planted in the fall.

According to the Old Farmer's Almanac, it's important when you plant, where you plant, and how you plant. The depth of soil, the right soil, the amount of sunlight, the right season, and the correct amount of moisture are all significant factors in growing healthy tulips. But once the bulb is planted, it's waiting time.

In our region, September is the time to plant your tulip bulbs. Then you wait for eight to nine months before you see the beauty of what was planted with much care and correctness. I'm sure you are understanding the analogy here. The vision that has been sown in your spirit by God takes time to grow. Don't be impulsive or careless with the vision God has implanted in you, nor grow weary before the beauty of that vision is evident to all.

Nehemiah waited patiently to approach the king with the Heavenly vision God had downloaded into him. In his time of waiting, he prayed, planned, and prepared for the next season of his life. Mark Elhardt says, "Preparation time is never wasted time." After the waiting season, Nehemiah was afraid to approach the king with his request (Nehemiah 2:2), but courage from the King of kings emboldened him. Our late President, Franklin D. Roosevelt, said, "Courage is not the absence of fear, but rather the assessment that something else is more important than fear." Nehemiah went beyond his fears because he saw the Heavenly vision. He went beyond the screams and into his dreams.

Action Steps

1. Establish prayer times everyday.
2. Ask God for a strategy that will move you closer to the vision.
3. Write down your goals, action steps, and dates in which you want the goal to be accomplished.

Goal: _____

_____

_____

Action Step: _____

_____

_____

Date Accomplished: _____

Goal: _____

_____

_____

Action Step: _____

_____

_____

Date Accomplished: _____

4. Meditate and Journal your thoughts on the following Scripture: "But they who wait for the LORD shall renew their strength; they shall mount up with wings like eagles; they shall run and not be weary; they shall walk and not faint" (Isaiah 40:31).

Notes

1. Derek Kidner, *Ezra And Nehemiah: An Introduction and Commentary*. Tyndale Old Testament Commentaries, Volume 12. General Editor: Donald J. Wiseman. (Downers Grove, IL: IVP Academic, 2009), 155.
2. Strong's H6960.

CHAPTER 7

GOING BEYOND THE SCREAMS

"And the king said to me, 'Why is your face sad, seeing you are not sick? This is nothing but sadness of the heart.' Then I was very much afraid."

(Nehemiah 2:2)

"I learned that courage was not the absence of fear, but the triumph over it. The brave man is not he who does not feel afraid, but he who conquers that fear."

(Nelson Mandela)

Fear is real. It was one of the first emotions felt by Adam and Eve after they chose the serpent's plan rather than God's. Some say fear is a spirit, "For God has not given us a spirit of fear, but of power and of love and of a sound mind" (2 Timothy 1:7, NKJV). Others say it's merely an emotion. I do know this much. Fear is real. I have used the acronym FEAR (False Evidence Appearing Real) to make the point that not all of our fears are justifiable. Often, we fear an outcome and play it out in our minds until we believe it's true. I get that. But fear is real. It's real in the sense that it can be felt and it often controls the behavior and decisions of people.

A real fear of mine is climbing ladders and riding roller coasters. I remember the first big roller coaster I rode on at Six Flags in Dallas, TX. My cousin, Tory, talked me into riding the roller coaster with him. I was petrified. Think about it. At any moment, the cars could derail and we would go flying into eternity. Or, we would be taking the fourth upside-down loop and I would projectile puke all over the people in front of me, or behind me, depending where I'm at in the loop. None of that happened! My stomach went up my chest and out my mouth, but I wasn't flung into eternity and I didn't vomit. Did I get over my fear? Maybe. Did I like to ride roller coasters? Not really. I prefer my feet on the ground.

For a very short period of time during my college years, I worked for a painter. Guess what? You have to use ladders! The guy I worked for climbed on ladders and roofs like a monkey. He had no fear. I was a lot more hesitant. Did I overcome my fear? Yes, I did. I became comfortable climbing ladders, until about twenty years later when I fell off my first ladder. I was on our front deck at my house in Aberdeen. The ladder slipped on the deck and I went flying. I can still feel the pain. Shortly after that episode, I fell off another ladder. The third time was the worst. I took a group of men to Sisseton, SD, to assist the Assembly of God Church with their new building. I climbed a ladder that was positioned against a wall. This wall was for a room that had a ceiling you could walk on. On the way up, the ladder slipped on the new cement and I grabbed the side of the wall and pulled myself up onto the platform. A new fear of ladders developed, introducing a fear that has controlled many of my decisions since.

My fear of roller coasters can't be substantiated by any horrendous experiences, but my fear of ladders can. Nehemiah's fear of the king was real. Though he faithfully served the king, approaching the king with sadness was not an acceptable posture for anyone. In the ancient days, to approach the king was a great honor, one that should be accompanied with great joy. But Nehemiah couldn't repress his true feelings any longer, so, when the king asked, "Why is your face sad, seeing you are not sick?" Nehemiah was immediately terrified. The fear of the unknown. The fear of approaching the king from a posture of weakness rather than strength and control. I can only imagine what Nehemiah was thinking, "Now what? What am I going to say? Will he punish me if I'm honest about my feelings? Will this be my last day on this planet?" The fear was real. It was substantiated. But Nehemiah went beyond the screams in his head. Fear may have gripped his soul, but it couldn't control him any longer. He went beyond the screams (fears) and into his dreams (God's Plan). He may have not approached the king boldly with joy, but he approached bravely with the stirrings of God.

Mark Twain said, "Courage is resistance to fear, mastery of fear—not absence of fear." Nehemiah felt the fear, but his fear was overcome when he chose to follow through with God's plan for his life. A God-given vision will always require you to have the courage to carry it out. You will face obstinate people. You will be misunderstood and questioned about your integrity and loyalty. You will have to make sacrifices of your time and money. And the good news is, that's just the beginning. Get over it! You will not please everyone nor should you! One of the biggest fears you will have to overcome is the fear of man. Scripture declares, "Fearing people is a dangerous trap, but trusting the LORD means safety" (Proverbs 29:25, NLT). I'm safest anywhere on this planet when I'm in the middle of God's will for my life.

Years ago, Christi and I went on a one-month sabbatical. I'm not sure one month qualifies for a sabbatical, but it was a much needed break nonetheless. The very first thing I began to hear from Heaven was, "Drew, you'll never fulfill your calling if you have the fear of man." I began to ponder that thought throughout our sabbatical. Paul Chappell says, "The fear of man strangles us, because we can never please everybody; but the fear of the Lord frees us, because it challenges us to live and serve for an audience of One." Fearing other people's opinion is binding and restricting. Why would we be more concerned about another man's view of us than with God's view?

Five days prior to our sabbatical, someone from our church falsely accused me and other people in our church of sinful things. I completely lost my peace. I wanted to run into a cave. I wanted to run and never come back. The pain is real for many pastors. We serve faithfully and then some disgruntled human being takes their rage out on a leader. My normal reaction is to fight back, but honestly, we were going on a sabbatical for a reason. We needed rest. Now I couldn't rest, and I had to answer questions from well-meaning people who were concerned. I began to fear and wonder, "What are people going to think? Are people going to think I'm taking a sabbatical for this reason? Will I even get a sabbatical now?" The worry train began to run down the track and the thoughts bombarding my mind became the fuel for that train.

Instead of running, I faced it by answering questions and confronting the lies with truth. So, going into the sabbatical, God began to deal with a deep-seated fear in my life, one concerning people's opinion of who I was or was not. Coming into a place of rest is very difficult for busybodies like me. I like to wake up early in the morning and get things done. Scratching my list off for the day is a sweet feeling. Accomplishing tasks is amazing! Resting, that's a drag, right? Do you ever stop what you're doing and ask the question, "Why am I keeping myself so busy?" Maybe us busybodies are afraid of the answer. Don't misunderstand me, I believe in hard work and remaining diligent. One of my love languages is "acts of service." Getting things done makes my heart smile. But, like anything else in this life, we get unbalanced.

About a month ago, I had a flat tire on Highway 281. Thankfully, I felt it pop and immediately was able to pull over on an approach and change it swiftly. I drove into Aberdeen with the spare and stopped at a place that specializes in tires. After checking the tires, the "Tire Doctors" found steel coming out of a few of them. With a deeper analysis, they found the tires to be unbalanced and out of alignment. When we get out of balance, what's inside begins to protrude and create a disruption in our lives. Being in alignment saves time and money. Being busy is honorable, but being out of balance with busyness is potentially harmful. What air we may have in our tires will leak out if we don't take the time to rest and become refreshed. But honestly, sometimes we're afraid of rest. When we rest, we're faced with our thoughts and fears. Busyness delays confrontation with our fears, becoming a way of escape.

Nehemiah waited four months to confront his greatest fear—revealing his feelings and communicating his vision for his homeland to the king. He was constrained by the fear of man. We can say he waited four months because, "It was God's perfect timing," and it may have been, but Nehemiah expresses the truth when he said, "Then I was very much afraid" (Nehemiah 2:2b). Nehemiah was afraid because it was counter-culture to express sadness or any emotion other than joy in the presence of the king. The last thing Nehemiah wanted was to lose favor with the king. Plus, Nehemiah was going to ask the king to reverse a decree that was already made (see Ezra 4:21).[1] The stakes were high for Nehemiah—share what's burning in my heart and possibly get rejected with a death sentence, or stay in my comfort zone where everything is safe. Hahaha! The safest place isn't the nest of fear but on the wings of God.

After God led his fearful people out of Egypt, He spoke to Moses on Mount Sinai, "You yourselves have seen what I did to the Egyptians, and how I bore you on *eagles' wings* and brought you to myself. Now therefore, if you will indeed obey my voice and keep my covenant, you shall be my treasured possession among all peoples, for all the earth is mine; and you shall be to me a kingdom of priests and a holy nation" (Exodus 19:4-6). God's plan for Israel was to make them His treasured possession, a kingdom of priests, and a holy nation. His plans were beautiful. His heart was huge for His people, His Family. Why did they disobey? Why did they rebel? Fear. John said it best, "There is no fear in love, but perfect love casts out fear. For fear has to do with punishment, and whoever fears has not been perfected in love" (1 John 4:8). They weren't perfected in love because they embraced their previous master, FEAR. Being slaves under horrible taskmasters will do that.

Good News Today—you are no longer a slave! You don't have to be in bondage to fear if you are a Child of God. "So you are no longer a slave, but a son, and if a son, then an heir through God" (Galatians 4:7). Here's more truth for those who are believers and followers of Jesus, "For you did not receive the spirit of slavery to fall back into fear, but you have received the Spirit of adoption as sons, by whom we cry, 'Abba! Father!'" Under the curse, we were subject to fear, but, "Christ redeemed us from the curse of the law by becoming a curse for us—for it is written, 'Cursed is everyone who is hanged on a tree'" (Galatians 3:13). I call those "Truth Bombs." They explode in your spirit and defeat the enemy that is attempting to keep you in bondage to fear.

There comes a time for every person with a God-given vision to confront his/her fears. Our late President, Harry S. Truman, said, "Men make history and not the other way around. In periods where there is no leadership, society stands still. Progress occurs when courageous, skillful leaders seize the opportunity to change things for the better." Will that courageous person be you? Will you rise up in this hour and take hold of your God-given vision? Will you confront your fears? You'll have to STOP MAKING EXCUSES! That fire in you may not be burning bright now, but stir it up a little and you'll find the fire is very much alive. Fear has been trying to snuff out your passion. Recognize the fear, confront the fear, kill the fear, then run strong with the vision in your heart! This is your time! This is your hour! This is a dawning of a NEW DAY!

Action Steps

1. Be honest with yourself. Answer this question, "Am I afraid to move forward with the vision for my life?" Journal your answer.
2. Ask God, "What is at the root of my fears?" Listen, then write.
3. Don't procrastinate. Deal with your fear today. Be honest with someone you trust about these fears inhibiting you. Ask them to pray for you.
4. Meditate and Journal your thoughts on the following Scripture: "Don't be pulled in different directions or worried about a thing. Be saturated in prayer throughout each day, offering your faith-filled requests before God with overflowing gratitude. Tell him every detail of your life, then God's wonderful peace that transcends human understanding, will make the answers known to you through Jesus Christ. So keep your thoughts continually fixed on all that is authentic and real, honorable and admirable, beautiful and respectful, pure and holy, merciful and kind. And fasten your thoughts on every glorious work of God, praising him always" (Philippians 4:6-8, TPT).

Notes

1. Derek Kidner, *Ezra And Nehemiah: An Introduction and Commentary*. Tyndale Old Testament Commentaries, Volume 12. General Editor: Donald J. Wiseman. (Downers Grove, IL: IVP Academic, 2009), 160-161.

CHAPTER 8

UNPRECEDENTED FAVOR WITH GOD

"And the king granted me what I asked, for the good hand of my God was upon me."

(Nehemiah 2:8b)

"Grace is the overflowing favor of God, and you can always count on it being available to draw upon as needed."

(Oswald Chambers)

When God births a vision in your heart, He doesn't work against you, He empowers you. Favor is the currency of Heaven to accomplish tasks on Earth. When God began to stir Nehemiah to action, He also released His favor to carry out His plans. Favor is bestowed upon us when we believe in Christ, and that favor grows in us when we learn to become a good steward of it. It's like faith. We've been given a measure of faith (Romans 12:3) and we learn to grow our faith through the hearing of God's Word, "So faith comes from hearing, and hearing through the word of Christ" (Romans 10:17). Faith comes from a seed. The Word of God is like a seed.

What is the Kingdom of God like? "The kingdom of heaven is like a grain of mustard seed that a man took and sowed in his field. It is the smallest of all seeds, but when it has grown it is larger than all the garden plants and becomes a tree, so that the birds of the air come and make nests in its branches" (Matthew 13:31-32). We're the stewards of the seed that has been sown into our hearts. We'll honor that seed and watch it grow, or we'll neglect it and see it diminish. We're the recipients of Heaven's seed and we're the stewards (see Matthew 13:3-8).

Our spirit and soul are like the garden for God's seed. The hard ground becomes broken up, the seed is planted, and we water and nourish that seed by removing the weeds. We become good stewards by guarding and protecting the seed. King Solomon wrote, "My son, be attentive to my words; incline your ear to my sayings. Let them not escape from your sight; keep them within your heart. For they are life to those who find them, and healing to all their flesh. Keep your heart with all vigilance, for from it flow the springs of life. Put away from you crooked speech, and put devious talk far from you" (Proverbs 4:20-24). Words are seeds. Seeds (words) take root and grow when we're alert and when we submit to them. We steward His words when they're at the center of our attention. The fruit of being a good steward of the seed is life and healing.

Jesus had the favor of God upon Him and He grew in that favor, "The Child continued to grow and become strong, increasing in wisdom; and the grace of God was upon Him" (Luke 2:40, NASB). The word "grace" is from the same Greek word, "charis,"[1] used for favor. We step into a dimension of favor when we become Christians, "For by grace you have been saved through faith. And this is not your own doing; it is the gift of God" (Ephesians 2:8). Once again, we've been given grace (favor) and we can grow in that grace (favor), "And Jesus kept increasing in wisdom and stature, and in favor with God and men" (Luke 2:52, NASB). The question remains, "How do we grow in favor with God and man?"

We increase in favor when we continue to keep the main thing, the main thing. Jesus told his parents, "Did you not see and know that it is necessary [as a duty] for Me to be in My Father's house and [occupied] about My Father's business?" (Luke 2:49, AMPC). We steward this gift of favor through continual relationship with God, and committing ourselves to His business. Here's another key, "And He went down with them and came to Nazareth and was [habitually] obedient to them" (Luke 2:51, AMPC). Jesus was habitually obedient to his earthly parents, wow! How do we steward favor? Through relationship and obedience.

The Prophet Samuel also experienced an increase in favor, "Now the boy Samuel continued to grow both in stature and in favor with the LORD and also with man" (1 Samuel 2:26). Samuel was increasing in favor, while his mentor was decreasing in favor. Samuel was under the tutelage of Eli the Priest. Eli had two wicked sons who did evil in the sight of God. The favor of God was not upon them because of their wickedness and rebellion against God's ways. A man of God came to Eli and said, "Why then do you scorn my sacrifices and my offerings that I commanded for my dwelling, and honor your sons above me by fattening yourselves on the choicest parts of every offering of my people Israel?" (1 Samuel 2:29). Eli was taking the choicest parts of the sacrifice, meant for God, and hoarding it for himself and his rebellious sons. Eli was honoring man over God, "For those who honor me I will honor, and those who despise me shall be lightly esteemed" (1 Samuel 2:30). God won't bless us with favor if we choose to rebel and honor man more than we honor Him.

Grace (favor) is a wonderful gift from God, but it's abused and wasted when we live in a place of rebellion and dishonor. We won't grow in favor when we have a distorted view of grace. Grace isn't our trump card that gets us out of our consistent acts of rebellion to God's Word. Joyce Meyer says, "Grace is not the freedom to sin; it is the power to live a holy life." Paul wrote to Titus, "For the grace of God has appeared, bringing salvation for all people, training us to renounce ungodliness and worldly passions, and to live self-controlled, upright, and godly lives in the present age, waiting for our blessed hope, the appearing of the glory of our great God and Savior Jesus Christ, who gave himself for us to redeem us from all lawlessness and to purify for himself a people for his own possession who are zealous for good works" (Titus 2:11-14). Grace is not only for our salvation, but also for our purification. Grace trains us to renounce ungodliness and embrace a life of purity in this present age. We believe a lie when we tell ourselves, "I'm just a sinner saved by grace and I can't help but sin." That lie empowers a life of sinfulness rather than empowering you to live an overcoming life.

Pastor Ron Enget says, "You're either a Saint or you Ain't." John wrote, "But to all who did receive him, who believed in his name, he gave the right to become children of God" (John 1:12). Peter wrote, "But you are a chosen race, a royal priesthood, a holy nation, a people for his own possession, that you may proclaim the excellencies of him who called you out of darkness into his marvelous light" (1 Peter 2:9). Paul wrote, "Therefore, if anyone is in Christ, he is a new creation. The old has passed away; behold, the new has come" (2 Corinthians 5:17). Each of these writers were inspired by the Holy Spirit to proclaim our new identity in Christ.

When Paul addressed the people of God in the opening of each of his letters, he didn't start out with, "To the sinners in Rome, Corinth, Galatia, Philippi, Colossae, or Thessalonica." No, he addressed them in accordance with their new identity in Christ. To the Romans he wrote, "To all those in Rome who are loved by God and called to be saints" (Romans 1:7). To the Corinthians, "To the church of God what is in Corinth, to those sanctified in Christ Jesus, called to be saints together" (1 Corinthians 1:2). To the Galatians, "To the churches of Galatia" (Galatians 1:2). To the Ephesians, "To the saints who are in Ephesus, and are faithful in Christ Jesus" (Ephesians 1:2). To the Philippians, "To all the saints in Christ Jesus who are at Philippi" (Philippians 1:1). To the Colossians, "To the saints and faithful brothers in Christ at Colossae" (Colossians 1:2). To the Thessalonians, "To the church of the Thessalonians in God the Father and the Lord Jesus Christ" (Thessalonians 1:1). Why is this important? When our identity is rooted in Christ and not Sin, which is death, we begin to live in accordance with our new nature, Life in Christ Jesus, and not our old nature, which is a life controlled by sin and death.

When we recognize our new identity in Christ, we become empowered to overcome sin. Truth no longer gives us permission to sin, nor does grace. The new covenant is so much greater than the old, "which is Christ in you, the hope of glory" (Colossians 1:27b). Because Christ is in us, we're no longer driven to sin, but compelled to live a life of holiness. Why would God command us to "be holy, for I am holy" (1 Peter 1:16) if He wouldn't give us the power through grace to be holy? That's absurd. What God commands us to do, He also provides the grace (empowerment) to do it. "Little children, you are from God and have overcome them, for he who is in you is greater than he who is in the world" (1 John 4:4). It's Christ in you that empowers you to live a life pleasing to God.

I'm not saying we'll never sin again, but I'm definitely not going to make allowances for sin by declaring, "Well, I'm just a sinner saved by grace and that's what sinners do, sin." John wrote, "If we confess our sins, he is faithful and just to forgive us our sins and to cleanse us from all unrighteousness" (1 John 1:9). John was writing to believers when he wrote this. James wrote to the church, "Therefore, confess your sins to one another and pray for one another, that you may be healed. The prayer of a righteous person has great power as it is working" (James 5:16). When we sin, confession is our connection to grace (favor). When we conceal sin, we begin to invite trouble rather than favor. "Whoever conceals their sins does not prosper, but the one who confesses and renounces them finds mercy" (Proverbs 28:13). For us to prosper in our God-given vision, it's important to quickly confess and renounce sin. The enemy (devil) would love to impede your progress. Remember, God is for you and has provided keys to unlock doors of favor. One of those keys is confession.

Nehemiah said, "...the good hand of my God was upon me" (Nehemiah 2:8). The hand of God is the favor of God. Nehemiah recognized where his favor came from: God. How did Nehemiah receive this favor? Nehemiah was a servant to the king, but more importantly, a servant of God. Do you remember his prayer recorded in chapter one of his book? "Let your ear be attentive and your eyes open, to hear the prayer of your servant that I now pray before you day and night for the people of Israel your servants, confessing the sins of the people of Israel, which we have sinned against you. Even I and my father's house have sinned" (Nehemiah 1:6). Nehemiah received a dimension of favor as one of God's children and grew in favor through his confession of sin and repentance.

Unprecedented favor is stewarded by a people who remain in continual fellowship with God. We remain in continual unbroken fellowship with God when we're quick to confess and renounce our sins. Nehemiah was quick to confess the sins of his people and take ownership of his own sins. He was demonstrating a heart of humility. Confession springs forth from a heart of humility. Walking in humility before God produces two things according to the Apostle Peter: more grace (favor) and promotion. "Clothe yourselves, all of you, with humility toward one another, for 'God opposes the proud but gives grace to the humble'" (1 Peter 5:5b). Our self-reliance, which is pride, puts God in opposition to us. Humility releases favor and more favor.

Humility sets us up for a timely promotion. "Humble yourselves, therefore, under the mighty hand of God so that at the proper time he may exalt you" (1 Peter 5:6). What did Nehemiah say? "...the good hand of my God was upon me" (Nehemiah 2:8). When we humble ourselves under God's hand, more grace is released, and favor and promotion materialize. When does promotion come? At the proper time. The Greek word used for "proper time" is "kairos." Kairos is the "opportune or seasonal time."[2] It's a "favorable moment."[3] After Nehemiah humbled himself, favor and promotion were released at the opportune time.

It's not God's sole responsibility to keep our vision in action. It's often contingent upon our humility. If we're not moving forward with the vision God has given us, it's important to examine why. Is God opposing us? Wait a second, I wrote God is for us. Why would I now even think He would be opposed to us? Ultimately, God is for us, and wants us to be fruitful and increase in this life, but God also opposes the proud. How does pride manifest? I'm going to narrow this down to two words. Self-reliance. The Merriam-Webster definition of self-reliance is: "reliance on one's own efforts and abilities." Paul wrote to the Philippians, "And I am sure of this, that he who began a good work in you will bring it to completion at the day of Jesus Christ" (Philippians 1:6). God began the good work in us and God will also finish it. Somewhere in the process, we try to take over.

When this prodigal came back to Christi in 1988, I was literally overcome by the Presence of God. I was submerged in His love. I was engulfed by God's grace. Words cannot describe the feeling I had that night in my dorm room when my Father God's Glory washed over me. I felt like I was transported from the pits of hell to Heaven's highest heights. I was so grateful to God for forgiving me and was literally speechless. I came into a new dimension of grace and quickly began to experience His favor upon my life. I felt unstoppable as I became a zealot for Jesus.

Do you remember the Scripture, "Enthusiasm without knowledge is no good; haste makes mistakes" (Proverbs 19:2, NLT)? Well, I had a ton of enthusiasm and very little knowledge. I made a lot of mistakes. Probably the biggest one was making vows to God such as, "I will never sin again. I will be the best Christian ever. I will, I will, I will." The middle letter in SIN is "I" for a reason. Humility and brokenness got me into His Presence, now I was trying to stay in it through my own strength. I became religious and rigid. My view on holiness was distorted. I thought I could become holy through my own strength. One of my favorite sayings was, "I must decrease, so He can increase." I had it backwards! I was misquoting the verse. John the Baptist said, "He must increase, but I must decrease" (John 3:30). Did you get the Divine order of this verse? He comes before I.

The Psalmist wrote, "You make known to me the path of life; in your presence there is fullness of joy; at your right hand are pleasures forevermore" (Psalm 16:11). The path of life is in God's Presence, not in trying to become Super Christian. When I tried to decrease myself first, the only thing that decreased was the joy of my salvation. What was I doing? I was relying on my willpower rather than His Power. I was trying to work out my salvation with fear and trembling (Philippians 2:12) while forsaking the following verse, "...for it is God who works in you, both to will and to work for his good pleasure" (Philippians 2:13). Bottom line, I was walking in self-reliance. I was full of pride. There's nothing like a few fiery trials that will take care of that. God is good!

The favor of God propels our Heavenly vision forward. Growing in favor with God happens through relationship with Him and obedience to Him. Everything in life flows through relationship. Billy Graham said, "Remember: he WANTS your fellowship, and He has done everything possible to make it a reality. He has forgiven your sins, at the cost of His own dear Son. He has given you His Word, and the priceless privilege of prayer and worship."[4] To know Him is to love Him. Our obedience flows out of our intimate relationship with Him. Henry Blackaby said it best, "God's commands are designed to guide you to life's very best. You will not obey Him, if you do not believe Him and trust Him. You cannot believe Him if you do not love Him. You cannot love Him unless you know Him." Simply put, if you walk with God, you'll step into His favor and fulfill His plans for your life.

Action Steps

1. Do you recognize the favor of God in your life?
2. How are you stewarding God's favor?
3. Ask God, "Have I been self-reliant in any area of my life? Am I fully trusting You?" Wait. Listen. Journal.
4. Meditate and Journal your thoughts on the following Scripture: "For the LORD God is a sun and shield; the LORD bestows favor and honor. No good thing does he withhold from those who walk uprightly" (Psalm 84:11).

Notes

1. Strong's 5485.
2. *Thayer's Greek Lexicon Electronic Database*, Blue Letter Bible, copyright © 2002, 2003, 2006, 2011 by Biblesoft, Inc., accessed November 5, 2019, www.blueletterbible.org.
3. *HELPS Word – Studies*, copyright © 1987, 2011 by Helps Ministries, Inc., accessed November 15, 2019, www.biblehub.com.
4. Billy Graham, *Hope for Each Day: Words of Wisdom and Faith*. (Nashville, TN: Thomas Nelson, 2017).

CHAPTER 9

UNPRECEDENTED FAVOR WITH PEOPLE

"And the king granted me what I asked, for the good hand of my God was upon me."

(Nehemiah 2:8b)

"Never let loyalty and kindness leave you! Tie them around your neck as a reminder. Write them deep within your heart. Then you will find favor with both God and people, and you will earn a good reputation."

(Proverbs 3:3-4)

The TV series, *Blue Bloods*, is a favorite of Christi and I. It's a great mix of action, suspense, and relational drama, with a pinch of humor. It's a series that depicts the fictional family, The Reagans, an Irish Catholic family who've been involved in police work for generations. Tom Selleck (Frank Reagan) is the main actor who plays the role of New York City's Police Commissioner. Frank's father was a former Commissioner and his two boys are police officers, while his daughter is the Assistant District Attorney. Every personality is distinct and strong.

One of my favorite characters is "Danny," played by Donnie Wahlberg. Danny is a fiery detective for the NYPD. He is the type of person who "pushes the envelope." He doesn't necessarily break the rules, but he certainly walks that "thin line" between right and wrong procedures to find and convict the culprit. Danny is pushy, opinionated, and strong. These qualities make him an excellent detective. These characteristics also generate plenty of enemies. But the one quality of Danny's character that sticks out the most is, he honors his father, Frank. At the end of every day, Danny knows who's boss, and he chooses to honor and respect him deeply.

Danny is strong, yet submissive. Not a quality you find in too many people. Strong personalities often attempt to make their own way, and push anyone out of the way to see their desires come to pass. Here's a good principle—RESPECT AND HONOR YOUR LEADERS AND GOD WILL PROMOTE YOU. If this is a difficult pill for you to swallow, maybe you need to watch a few episodes of *Blue Bloods*! I understand, some leaders can abuse their authority and become more like dictators, rather than servants. If you're in an abusive leadership model that manipulates, controls, and makes constant demands, you may want to consider fleeing rather than clinging to this model. In most cases, though, strong personality people are continuously invited by God to learn the ways of Christ.

> In your relationships with one another, have the same mindset as Christ Jesus: Who, being in very nature God, did not consider equality with God something to be used to his own advantage; rather, he made himself nothing by taking the very nature of a servant, being made in human likeness. And being found in appearance as a man, he humbled himself by becoming obedient to death—even death on a cross!
>
> (Philippians 2:5-8, NIV)

Choosing the Ancient Paths of Christ never becomes irrelevant in any generation. The path of humility always wins in the end. Trying to make a way for ourselves and pushing ourselves to the front of the line always demotes us to the back of the line.

1992 was a great year for me. In February, I was set free by the Power of God from depression and discouragement. In June, July, and August, I interned as a Youth Pastor in Lemmon, SD. During that internship, I saw God's Power touch people's lives and I had the opportunity to preach seven times. It was life-changing, as God was beginning to build my confidence and teaching me to never forsake my small beginnings. Then September rolled around and so did my last quarter of college. December of 1992 was my last month of school at Moorhead State University. What a great year!

I received a phone call in December from June Becker. June was my dad's first cousin who was a fiery Evangelist in the '40s, '50s, '60s, and '70s. In 1992, June was on staff as a visitation pastor in Baltimore, MD. I hadn't heard from June since the early '80s, so I was shocked when she called and said, "I have been praying for you, and believe God wants you to come to Baltimore and be our Youth Pastor." I said, "Well, I don't think so. I'm starting an internship at First Assembly in Fargo, in January." She was persistent as usual, but I had plans. About a week later, I found out the internship in Fargo wouldn't start until the month of June. I went to Baltimore for four months. I guess June Becker had more favor with God than I did.

What could God possibly do in four months? My attempts at trying to figure out how God moves are hilarious. We're trained to use logic and reasoning, but in the Kingdom, we better submit to being "led by the Spirit" (Romans 8:14). I knew I was on an assignment, but quickly discovered the assignment was geared to get me into alignment. Have you ever driven a car with a manual transmission, better known as a "stick shift"? I had a Ford Tempo with "four on the floor." My first few attempts at shifting were rough. We used to say, "grind them 'til you find them." My time in Baltimore was similar to driving a manual transmission car, where I had to grind some things out in my own personality and character before I found the flow. I prayed a lot!

Not everything in Baltimore was a grinding experience. In one of our powerful morning prayer meetings, I sensed the Presence and Power of God. Along with that supernatural strength, I was given supernatural knowledge (1 Corinthians 12:8) about someone suffering with oppression, which was being experienced generationally in their family. A woman, by the name of Marion, said it was her. I asked her if I could pray for her. When she said "yes," something happened supernaturally. Marion let out a scream, and then she wept profusely.

It was dramatic and powerful! She later wrote me a letter, saying, "Marion is Free!" She got delivered from this generational oppression that had been emotionally tormenting her for years. God is good!

After this experience and a few others, I wanted to learn more about the Believer's Authority in Christ. I wanted to learn how we have authority over demons and how to minister freedom to those bound with oppression. One day I was walking in the downtown area of Baltimore and I stumbled across a Christian bookstore. As I was looking at titles of books, I found one that had "Authority" on the front cover. I thought to myself, "That looks like a good book on authority over demons." Little did I know, the book was more about rebellion and honoring the leaders in our life. I was a little disappointed at first, but endured the first few chapters, and then found myself on my face before God crying out, "God forgive me and help me!" The gears began to grind.

I grew up in Aberdeen, South Dakota. Aberdeen is a great place! My childhood memories are plenty and mostly happy. All of us grow up in a particular culture that's infused with a specific language, attitude, favorite foods, clothing style, and an unrealized expectation of "this is how we do life here." Church life has a culture too. Oftentimes, we're unaware of how much the culture of the community has influenced the culture of our church. Paul wrote, "Stop imitating the ideals and opinions of the culture around you, but be inwardly transformed by the Holy Spirit through a total reformation of how you think. This will empower you to discern God's will as you live a beautiful life, satisfying and perfect in his eyes" (Romans 12:2, TPT). The Holy Spirit is our mentor who has inspired the Holy Writ, the Bible. Holy Spirit knows the culture of Heaven. God's inspired Word reveals the culture of Heaven. Heaven's culture is to be admired, honored, and experienced here on this Earth. Didn't Jesus teach us how to pray? "Your kingdom come, your will be done, on earth as it is in heaven" (Matthew 6:10). With His Kingdom comes His culture—the culture of Heaven.

Aberdeen is a community filled with some of the greatest people on the planet. I love my city! We may be small, but we think and dream big. We have some of the greatest pastors in our churches and the unity is rising amongst us like never before. However, like any community, not everything is perfect. Hey,

I should know, I live here! Recently, our church hosted a conference called "ROAR!" Our guest speaker was Bobby Conner. Bobby grew up in Texas and is celebrating fifty years in faithful ministry. He's well-traveled and has experienced hundreds of different cultures on the Earth. He's also well-traveled in the spiritual sense. He's extremely sensitive to God's voice and the plans of God for future events. You could say, "Bobby is a Prophet." That VeggieTales song just popped into my head:

> Jonah was a prophet
> Oo-ooh!
> But he really never got it
> Sad but true!
> And if you watch him you can spot it
> A-doodley-doo!
> He did not get the point![1]

Thankfully, Bobby isn't like the Prophet Jonah. He gets the point!

I asked Bobby while he was here, "What spirit affects Aberdeen in a negative way? What spirit attempts to rule our culture?" Bobby's response was illuminating. He said without hesitation, "Self-reliance, and the root is pride." Ouch! I was quickly reminded of a teaching I heard years ago from Dr. David Nichols. David said there's two prevailing cultures that inhabit our region (which includes North Dakota, South Dakota, and Minnesota), the German Culture and the Scandinavian Culture. Dr. Nichols said both have two prevailing creeds. The German Creed is, "Übermensch," which means, "Superman." The German Philosopher, Friedrich Nietzsche, coined this term in 1883, as recorded in the dictionary at Vocabulary.com. Described in Urbandictionary. com, "Nietzsche begins his premise with the assumption that God does not exist, and if God does not exist, thus objective morality and inherent value are not possible since there is no ultimate being that exists to create morality and value in the first place." In other words, it's the opposite of Jesus Christ and it's all about becoming self-reliant, rather than being reliant upon God.

How does it manifest in our everyday lives? Have you ever heard, "Where there's a will, there's a way," "Pull yourself up by your bootstraps," or perhaps,

"If I don't do it, no one will"? Words are powerful. If we find their origins, we may find which culture is empowering them and impacting us. Words affect attitudes, and attitudes and words create culture. Growing up in Aberdeen, I found this to be true. Some of our favorite sayings were, "Suck it up," "You're a wimp," "Be a man!" My language was centered around how strong I could be, not how powerful God is. When I went through the fiery trials in the early '90s, the first thing God dealt with was my speech. I heard this phrase in my spirit, "The tune of your tongue reveals the tone of your heart." Jesus said, "For it is out of the abundance of the heart that the mouth speaks" (Luke 6:45). Words become indicators or locators of what's happening in our hearts.

My early years of ministry were transformational moments that God used to establish me for years to come. "But the Lord is faithful. He will establish you and guard you against the evil one" (2 Thessalonians 3:3). I learned a valuable lesson in Baltimore, MD. I learned that God has established some people to be in a position of authority, and it's not always me. I was young, opinionated, and at times very narrow-minded. On spiritual gifts tests, I don't score high in mercy. My pastor in Baltimore had a personality like mine. He would be considered a strong "D" on the DISC Profile Test. "D" personalities are determined, bold, and opinionated. God used my pastor to refine me. I came under the Mighty Hand of God and allowed Him to shape me into the man He desired me to be. I learned to listen and obey. I didn't agree with everything the pastor wanted me to do, but I learned to submit my agendas and support the vision of the pastor. The things I didn't agree with were methodological, not ethical.

When I was growing up, the church culture wasn't always in alignment with the Culture of God's Kingdom. The pastor often didn't have what I call, "Visional Authority." I would define Visional Authority as: someone called by God to lead through God's Grace, love, and plan for a specific group of people. The visionary leader would be led by the Spirit of God, not by the opinions and agendas of people. Not all pastors have this authority and the reasons vary: (1) it's not the model of the church, (2) the pastor has relinquished his/her authority, and (3) the church has experienced a frequent turnover of pastoral leadership, so some people within the ranks have assumed that place of authority and refuse to relinquish it unto the pastor. Whatever the reason may be, I experienced this prior to coming to Baltimore, and God wasn't allowing me to carry it with me to my next assignment.

Nehemiah had favor with the king. I'm 100 percent convinced that his favor came from God first, but grew with man because of his humility and loyalty. King Solomon wrote, "Never let loyalty and kindness leave you! Tie them around your neck as a reminder. Write them deep within your heart. Then you will find favor with both God and people, and you will earn a good reputation" (Proverbs 3:3-4). Favor grows when we steward it through loyalty and kindness. Nehemiah developed a friendship with the king when he risked his own life everyday as the cupbearer. Nehemiah kept the king safe and was kind and loyal throughout his position as the cupbearer. So, when God spoke to Nehemiah, he had relational equity with the king, and therefore found favor for his next assignment.

Young pastors, listen to me. Do you want to fulfill the vision of God for your life? I'm going to assume your answer right now is "yes!" Young business person or entrepreneur, do you want to impact your generation for the Glory of God? I hear your "yes!" Here it is—learn to submit yourself to the leadership God has given you. Learn to serve. You'll never father or mother a younger generation someday until you learn to be a good son or daughter today. I remember the zeal and ambition I had in my twenties and thirties. It was contagious. It was also dangerous without my willingness to submit myself to my God-given leaders.

My assignment in Baltimore was short, but it ended in honor. I was asked to stay as the full-time Youth Pastor, but God's plan for me was to come back to the Dakotas. When I talk about submitting, I'm not suggesting you allow your leaders to control you. Some leaders struggle with control, I get it. I'm encouraging you to be a servant to your leader through loyalty and kindness. I'm discouraging you from starting a coup against your leader because you think your way is the right way. I had people at the church in Baltimore approach me with their complaints against the pastor. What do you do with that? You don't entertain it or come into agreement with it. You encourage them to talk to their leader. In some cases, not in Baltimore, the leader is unapproachable and controlling. This may be a good reason for you to find a safe place to grow.

Maybe it's time to move on, and then ask God to have mercy on the leader and heal them of their hurts.

Here's the bottom line: the way up is the way down. You'll never lead in the capacity God desires for you without learning the Ancient Paths of humility and servanthood. "Great leaders do not desire to lead but to serve" (Myles Munroe). Nehemiah received unprecedented favor from God and man, then he learned to be a great steward of that favor through his loyalty to God and his loyalty, friendship, and kindness to his leader, the king. Don't allow pride to rise up and rob you of your destiny. Take action through the posture of humility and you will align yourself with God's unprecedented favor that overcomes obstacles and your enemies.

Action Steps

1. Define humility in your own words.
2. Be honest with yourself. Ask, "Have I honored leaders in my life? Have I been obedient or rebellious?"
3. Renounce pride. Embrace humility and loyalty. If you desire to create a culture of honor in your life, write down your commitment as a declaration of how you want to live. For example:

    I will honor and respect authority figures in my life. I will pray for them and speak blessing and not cursing over them. I will respect them to their face and behind their back. I will walk in humility and allow God to promote me. I embrace humility and renounce selfish ambition.

4. Meditate and Journal your thoughts on the following Scripture: "Never let loyalty and kindness leave you! Tie them around your neck as a reminder. Write them deep within your heart. Then you will find favor with both God and people, and you will earn a good reputation" (Proverbs 3:3-4).

Notes

1. David Mullen and Phil Vischer, "Jonah Was a Prophet," *Jonah: A Veggie Tales Movie*. Who'S Jo, Who'S Jo Music, 2002, compact disc.

CHAPTER 10

RESISTANCE

"But when Sanballat the Horonite and Tobiah the Ammonite servant heard this, it displeased them greatly that someone had come to seek the welfare of the people of Israel."

(Nehemiah 2:10)

"Sometimes new opportunity means new opposition. Not everything God asks us to do will be comfortable."

(Joyce Meyer)

Resistance is often a sign that you're headed in the right direction. Motion invites resistance. If I run around a track, the wind is at my back for a portion of the race but then resists me at other locations. If I lift weights, resistance is valuable in building muscle. If I have no resistance when lifting, I have no gain. Water makes it possible for us to swim, and with every stroke comes resistance. Get over it, you will have resistance when you move forward in your God-given vision. It's inevitable and it's valuable. Jon Gordon says, "When you experience resistance, you find the lessons that you are meant to learn." Resistance is an opportunity to clarify your vision and strengthen your resolve.

Possessing favor with God and with man doesn't exclude you from resistance. The Psalmist declared, "Many are the afflictions of the righteous, but the LORD delivers him out of them all" (Psalm 34:19). Nehemiah had favor with God and with man, but not all men. When Sanballat and Tobiah heard of Nehemiah and his quest to help the Jews, they were anything but pleased. Some will celebrate your presence and others barely tolerate it. Jesus was even rejected in His homeland. Don't let rejection stop or discourage you.

During my college years, I met Peter Mehl, a mighty man of God. Pete came to church in a sharp suit, a cool hat, and he drove a sweet car. He was a successful businessman who knew how to pray. He and his wife, Jill, were sold out for Jesus. In the early '90s, Pete began to be stirred by God to reach Ukraine for Christ. The Iron Curtain had come down and people were starting to spread the Gospel in unreached areas of the world. He and Jill sold all they had and moved their entire family to Ukraine. They left a lucrative business and a very comfortable lifestyle to reach Ukraine for Christ.

They came to a land that was spiritually dark, dry, and somewhat hostile to the Gospel. Though people came to Christ, the Mehls experienced some major resistance. They were chased, shot at, and despised for the cause of Christ. The first couple years were especially difficult as they encountered the Russian Mafia, faced death threats, were robbed, and interrogated by the KGB. They met much resistance. Pete was probably one of the boldest guys I've ever met. He was a bulldog for Jesus. The resistance they faced gave Pete and Jill a greater resolve in their spirit to finish what God had started through them.

In 2010, I had the opportunity to go to Ukraine and minister with the Mehls. Because of their perseverance, they've literally seen thousands upon thousands of people come to Christ. They have connections all over the Nations of Ukraine, Moldova, and the Crimean Peninsula. The Mehls have started hundreds of churches, trained fifteen thousand students, launched Bible Schools, missionary training centers, and started a drug rehab center. I had the opportunity to preach in various locations and see God touch hundreds of lives. One of the most memorable experiences was preaching in the highest security prison in Ukraine. These men were receiving Christ and praising Him for His goodness. It was beautiful!

Persistence takes us beyond the pain of resistance and allows us to eat the fruit of our perseverance. Woody Hayes says, "Paralyze resistance with persistence." I can't imagine what would've happened to thousands of souls had the Mehls decided to give up during the early years. They could've said, "This is too dangerous for our family. We have to leave and never come back." I don't think a person on the planet would have blamed them. But not Peter and Jill. They fought the good fight of faith because they saw the Heavenly vision before them. They were burning with Heaven's passion that fueled them through any opposition the enemy threw at them. They never gave up and now are eating the fruit of their labors. Many people are rejoicing in Ukraine and surrounding areas because Peter and Jill Mehl decided not to give up or give in to the resistance.

At this very moment, Pete is rejoicing in Heaven. His Savior has welcomed him with a "job well done, My good and faithful servant." He went to his Heavenly home on May 11th of 2017. He was an Apostle, a sent one from Jesus. He was a messenger to a people who were in darkness, but who now have come to THE LIGHT! Jill is still ministering in Ukraine and the family has continued the legacy of persistence against resistance. What a legacy! What a blessing!

Nehemiah was a sent one. He was on a mission to complete the construction of the walls around Jerusalem. He came back to the homeland of his forefathers to protect his countrymen and to finish the work God had sent him to accomplish. Resistance came through political leaders of that region, but nothing would stop Nehemiah. Why? He heard from Heaven. As Nehemiah was surveying Jerusalem, he wrote, "Then I arose in the night, I and a few men with me. And I told no one what my God had put into my heart to do for Jerusalem" (Nehemiah 2:12). The fire of God's breath was residing in Nehemiah. He was branded with Heaven's vision. He wouldn't allow anything or anyone to deter him from finishing what God had started in him.

Two particular characters became adversaries to Nehemiah and the Jews, and they were Sanballat and Tobiah. These men were influential and had a vast array of connections in and around Jerusalem.[1] Throughout Nehemiah's mission to rebuild the walls, Sanballat and Tobiah attempted to frustrate Nehemiah and the Jews. Their goal was to completely stop the building. If they could stop the building, Jerusalem would be unprotected from her enemies and would remain vulnerable to attack. They didn't want to lose any control nor did they want to see the reemergence of the Jews in Jerusalem.

The book of Nehemiah records the various reactions of Sanballat and Tobiah:

1. They were displeased when they heard Nehemiah came to help the people of Israel (Nehemiah 2:10).
2. They ridiculed, scorned, and despised Nehemiah and the Jews. They questioned Nehemiah's motives and asked him, "Will you rebel against the king?" (Nehemiah 2:20).
3. They were in great rage and continued to ridicule the Jews with mockery and insults (Nehemiah 4:1-3).
4. They formed an alliance with the Arabians, Ammonites, and Ashdodites. The demonic alliance plotted together to fight against Jerusalem, to bring injury and cause confusion (Nehemiah 4:8).
5. Their anger turned to wrath. They wanted to kill the Jews (Nehemiah 4:11).
6. They falsely accused Nehemiah. They sent threats to weaken his hands and attempted to strike fear into his heart (Nehemiah 6:5-13).

Once again, resistance is often a sign that you're headed in the right direction. Sometimes, the greater the purpose, the more vocal our enemy becomes. If you take time to think about the attacks, you'll discover how the enemy is revealing himself and his fears. He "shows his hand" so you can pray strategically. Also, notice the progression of attacks. Sanballat and Tobiah went from displeasure to scorn, scorn to rage, from rage to forming a coup to bring confusion, rage to death threats, and then their last straw was to release false accusations. If you look back to the book of Ezra, you'll discover the same pattern of attacks against God's People when they began to rebuild the Temple. "Then the people of the land tried to discourage the people of Judah. They troubled them in building, and hired counselors against them to frustrate their purpose all the days of Cyrus king of Persia, even until the reign of Darius king of Persia" (Ezra 4:4-5, NKJV). They attempted to discourage, trouble, and frustrate the people of God. When that didn't work, "...they wrote an accusation against the inhabitants of Judah and Jerusalem" (Ezra 4:6). Our adversary doesn't want God's vision for your life to come to fruition. He doesn't want you to possess any more ground, therefore, he attempts to wear you down with discouragement, trouble, and false accusations.

It's important to be aware of your enemy. Paul wrote to the Church of Corinth, "so that we would not be outwitted by Satan; for we are not ignorant of his designs" (2 Corinthians 2:11). What's equally important is our response to his attacks. How did Nehemiah respond?

1. He moved forward with his plans (Nehemiah 2:11).
2. He declared truth. "The God of heaven will make us prosper, and we his servants will arise and build, but you have no portion or right or claim in Jerusalem" (Nehemiah 2:20).
3. He prayed and continued to build the wall (Nehemiah 4:4-6).
4. He rallied others to pray and then set a guard to protect the wall (Nehemiah 4:9).
5. He strategically positioned people by their clans and equipped them with weapons (Nehemiah 4:13).
6. He told his people, "Do not be afraid of them" (Nehemiah 4:14).
7. He directed their attention to God (Nehemiah 4:14).
8. He reminded the laborers who they were building for (Nehemiah 4:14).
9. He repositioned the workers, some building and others standing with spears, shields, and bows (Nehemiah 4:16).
10. He discerned the enemies' tactics and would not stop working on the wall (Nehemiah 6:2-3).
11. He responded to the accusations with truth and discerned the enemies' attempt to stop the work (Nehemiah 6:8-9).
12. He prayed (Nehemiah 6:14).

When you begin to take action with the vision God has entrusted to you, resistance will inevitably come. Nehemiah never quit because he had a reservoir of truth inside of him. That reservoir of truth was built up during his times of waiting and praying. Do you remember the four months he waited to approach the king? How about his journey from Iran to Jerusalem? Then his three days of surveying and examining the condition of Jerusalem? God had been preparing Nehemiah for any obstacle he may face. The same is true for you today. You may be facing resistance, but God has given you a promise, and with that promise, He has given you the anointing, equipment, and courage to break through the resistance! Finish strong my friend! Activate your God-given persistence and overcome the resistance. You will not regret it.

Action Steps

1. In what ways are you experiencing resistance?
2. What is your plan to overcome resistance?
3. Repeat the practice of writing goals, establishing action steps, and setting deadlines for your goals to be accomplished.

Goal: _____

_____

_____

Action Step: _____

_____

_____

Date Accomplished: _____

Goal: _____

_____

_____

Action Step: _____

_____

_____

Date Accomplished: _____

1. Meditate and Journal your thoughts on the following Scripture: "And let us not grow weary of doing good, for in due season we will reap, if we do not give up" (Galatians 6:9).

Notes

1. Derek Kidner and Donald J. Wiseman, *The Tyndale Old Testament commentaries. An Introduction and Commentary on Books I and II of the Psalms.* (Leicester: Inter-Varsity Press, 1979), 164-165.

CHAPTER 11

REVIEW THE SITUATION

"Then I said to them, you see the bad situation we are in—how Jerusalem lies in ruins, and its gates are burned with fire. Come, let us build up the wall of Jerusalem, that we may no longer be a disgrace."

(Nehemiah 2:17 AMPC)

"Panic causes tunnel vision. Calm acceptance of danger allows us to more easily assess the situation and see the options."

(Simon Sinek)

December 7, 1941 was described by President Franklin D. Roosevelt as, "A date which will live in infamy." It was the day Pearl Harbor was attacked by the Japanese. The United States had been preparing for a possible war with Japan, but wasn't prepared for the aerial attack that brought utter devastation to the islands in the Pacific. It's hard to imagine, but try to imagine with me being on the beautiful Island of Oahu, then suddenly being awakened by bombs going off. The attack started at 7:55 a.m. and lasted about an hour and fifteen minutes. I'm sure it seemed to last a lifetime as 353 of Japan's aircraft flew over with bombs, torpedoes, and the emergence of the Kamikaze flyers.

The destruction that day was immense. According to Census.gov, Americans who died from the attacks numbered 2,403. All were in the military except for 68 civilians. The number of wounded was 1,178. Between the Army Air Corp and Navy, 159 aircraft were damaged and 169 destroyed. Amongst the

Battleships, Cruisers, Destroyers, and Auxiliary ships, 16 were severely damaged and 3 were completely destroyed. Almost complete devastation. Needless to say, after the attack, America was awakened and immediately entered what we now know as World War II. Our next step was to assess the damage and then move forward with a counterattack that would become known as "The Battle of Midway." It was America's plan to stop Japan from attacking the West Coast of the United States. I'm grateful the plan worked and we stopped further destruction.

But prior to the battle at Midway, we had to make an assessment of the damages before we could move on. Taking time to review difficult situations is imperative in order to move forward strategically with the vision God has given you. Like Pearl Harbor, Jerusalem was in a very difficult season, one that may have appeared to be hopeless. Nehemiah said, "You see the bad situation we are in—how Jerusalem lies in ruins, and its gates are burned with fire. Come, let us build up the wall of Jerusalem, that we may no longer be a disgrace" (Nehemiah 2:17, AMPC). Nehemiah assessed the destruction, and it stirred him to action. He basically said, "Enough is enough! Let's take action and take action NOW!" Like the U.S. after Pearl Harbor, Nehemiah assessed the situation and moved forward with the vision to protect his people.

Reviewing our present condition may be very difficult, but necessary. We often have the tendency to form an attitude that reflects our thinking, "If it's not affecting me in a negative way, why should I be concerned?" The problem with that thinking is this: if we don't confront the little problems, they won't remain little, they will grow. America's issues with Japan didn't begin at Pearl Harbor, they escalated over several years and we found ourselves sleeping when the attack finally occurred. Jerusalem's walls (protection) weren't a new problem. They had been charred and lying down in ruins for over a hundred and fifty years since their destruction, and it had been around ninety to one hundred years since Zerubbabel began work on the foundation of the Temple. It was disgraceful to Nehemiah that no one finished what had been started.

Here's some great news! Are you ready? God finishes what He starts! It was a hot day in Dallas, Texas, when I was struggling to break free from personal pain and a mind full of doubts. I woke up early in the morning to attend a prayer meeting at a church I had never darkened the doors of. After the prayer meeting, a pastor on staff gave me a ride back to my hotel and then prayed with me. The pastor said, "I have a word for you. It's Philippians 1:6, 'being confident of this, that he who began a good work in you will carry it on to completion until the day of Christ Jesus.'" I was elated! I had just read that verse a few days before the pastor spoke it over my life. Wow, what a promise! It's true, the work He begins, He completes. Here's another truth: revival begins with me. Before I can repair the broken-down walls of our society, I must take time to evaluate my own life and discover my need for renewal and repair.

Walls represent protection, either good or bad. When someone is cold and "stand-offish," we say, "They have walls around them." The proverbial walls are blockades we have manufactured in our mind and emotions to keep other people from knowing and seeing who we really are. They have been created for protection—protection from further hurt and wounds. Have you ever seen an abused dog? They snarl, growl, and bite anyone who attempts to come close. If their former master was abusive, they translate that into, "Every human is abusive and I must protect myself."

Do you have walls around your heart? Do you know why? Have you discovered the source of your pain and how it affects you daily? Don't get me wrong, I believe in healthy boundaries. Without them we can never fully function in the vision God has entrusted us with. Nehemiah had boundaries. He didn't let his enemies work with him. He refused to meet with his enemies when they wanted to meet with him, lest they discourage him and sway him to stop building the wall (Nehemiah 5:1-9). Boundaries are healthy and they're necessary. Not every one of your relationships will require heavy-duty boundaries, but some definitely will. With your close and trusted friends, the boundaries look more like a fence with a front gate.

Wounds don't just dissipate into thin air, they must be acknowledged and properly attended to. Denial is a real problem for many people. The reaction for some is fight and for others, flight. The majority of the people I've met choose flight. They choose to run from the problem rather than face it. This person has what I call "Ostrichitis." Ostrichitis is a condition that forms when you continue to stick your head in the sand and refuse to face the issues of your heart. It's scary to admit your hurt. It's even scarier to communicate your pain with the person or persons who created the pain in you. Unless you pull your head out of the sand, you won't be able to see clearly. Does your vision seem stuck? Do you feel stuck? Maybe you are. It might be time to deal with the hurts before they deal with you. It's okay to evaluate. Part of the process of putting your vision into action is confronting yourself. Be honest about the pain. Stop building walls. Your spiritual, emotional, mental, and physical well-being is dependent upon your willingness to be honest.

Growing up is hard to do. Throughout my early years, I was a "stuffer." I stuffed everything inside and refused to be completely honest and transparent about what was really going on inside of me. I was stuck. I had to locate the root of my pain. Have you ever had to dig a hole or excavate on your property? In South Dakota, the number to call is 811. They'll connect with local power companies or utility companies to come to your property and locate underground utilities, then they mark the location of those utilities with spray paint and little plastic flags. The flags serve as indicators of where the utilities are underground. Our emotions serve us as indicators. John and Paula Sanford said, "Trace the fruit to the root." Our emotions can deceive us, but if we're attuned, they can indicate to us what is affecting our attitudes and our perspective. Our emotions can be the flags that indicate what's going on under the surface.

I have served in full-time ministry for over twenty-five years. After a few short years, you begin to discover much about the psyche and emotions of the people you're ministering to. I have a saying, "The issue is often not the issue." We're not always the best at locating the source of our frustrations. Why? Here's maybe a few reasons:

1. We're afraid to be completely honest. Sometimes the truth is too painful.
2. We have "stuffed" our feelings down for so long, we can't locate the original offense.
3. We grew up in a family dynamic that wouldn't allow us to express our true thoughts and feelings.

4.   We're afraid of what others may think of us, so we remain in denial that something could be wrong.
5.   We have taken the position that all emotions are bad, therefore I can't allow my emotions to affect me in any way.
6.   Some have been taught, "It's not faith to feel."
7.   We have learned to masquerade the real issue of our heart with other issues. We "beat around the bush" rather than going to the root of the matter.

Okay, that was more than a few reasons. Whatever category you find yourself in, it's important to locate the source of pain so you can become a healthy and whole person. You may be extremely gifted in your profession, but don't allow yourself to hide behind your giftedness. It's time to be free from the pain! You don't need to be locked up inside anymore. God has given you emotions as indicators for you to be able to evaluate how you're doing, and not only your emotions, but also your words. Jesus said, "For out of the abundance of the heart his mouth speaks" (Luke 6:45b). The tune of your tongue reveals the tone of your heart. It's okay to recognize you are hurting. It's not okay to stay stuck in that hurt. Many plans and purposes have been aborted in people's lives due to being stuck in pain.

Your perspective becomes cloudy when you're offended and stuck in the pain. The big and exciting vision slowly becomes faded in the fog of frustration. Your focus is no longer on the big picture but the little pebble in your shoe. Stop! Take off your shoe and shake the pebble out! Take the time to invest in your own mental and emotional self, you won't regret it. Seasons of evaluation are extremely important. If you want to run with the vision, you sometimes need to walk slowly with the vision so you can catch your breath. Have you ever sought wise counsel? Either from mentors, pastors, or professional counselors? I suggest you seek them out, especially if you're stuck in the mud of your emotions.

If we don't confront our pain, our pain will confront us. "What's the big deal?" you may ask. You are the big deal. Your health is the big deal. God's vision for your life is the big deal. The people you're meant to bring life to are the big deal. Your spouse is the big deal. Your children are the big deal. Your friends and family are the big deal. Don't wait another day! Get some help! Get some counsel. Your future depends on it. Grab hold of your destiny by embracing change.

When you refuse to confront the pain, you begin to view life through another lens. Everything becomes filtered through your pain. You may be able to smile on Sunday, but Monday comes and you find yourself in the mud. As Christians, we're told countless times, "Don't live on your emotions, live on the Word of God." I agree! But, if you don't allow your emotions to become indicators and signals for the pain residing and growing in your heart, you'll not only live on your emotions, you'll be completely controlled by them.

We're made in the image of God (Genesis 1:27). God is a spirit (John 4:24) and He has emotions. His emotions are completely pure, but He has emotions. God has been described with the following characteristics and emotions:

1. Love (Psalm 36:7; Micah 7:18; Romans 5:5).
2. Grief (Isaiah 63:10; Ephesians 4:30).
3. Jealousy (Deuteronomy 4:24; Joshua 24:19).
4. Kindness (Romans 2:4; Titus 3:4).
5. Joy (Nehemiah 8:10; Zephaniah 3:17; Romans 14:17).
6. Compassion (Matthew 9:36; James 5:11).

The above is not an exhaustive list, but an example of God possessing emotions. He certainly doesn't have "mood swings" like we may have, but He does have a personality. Emotions aren't bad, they are good. God gave us emotions to enjoy life, express love, and assist us in locating what's happening internally.

Jesus is our perfect example of living a whole life on planet Earth. He was rejected and denied by many, falsely accused, run out of town, and eventually whipped thirty-nine times, nailed to a cross, and crowned with thorns. While on Earth, He was fully God and fully man. He endured great hardship and felt the array of emotions that you and I do. Jesus was able to overcome through love, compassion, forgiveness, kindness, and healing. How did He do it? When tempted in the Wilderness by Satan, He said, "It is written" (Matthew 4:4). Jesus lived on the Word of God, "Man shall not live by bread alone, but by every word that comes from the mouth of God" (Matthew 4:4). Jesus did what He saw His Father doing, "Truly, truly, I say to you, the Son can do nothing of his own accord, but only what he sees the Father doing. For whatever the Father does, that the Son does likewise" (John 5:19). Jesus was busy, but never too busy to prioritize His life around the Presence of His Father, "And rising very early in the morning, while it was still dark, he departed and went out to a desolate place, and there he prayed" (Mark 1:35). The key to being unstuck in your emotions is found in the Presence of God and the Word of God.

Toxicity begins to build up in our lives when we don't prioritize our lives around God's Presence and His Word. The Psalmist said, "I am afflicted very much; Revive me, O LORD, according to Your word" (Psalm 119:107). To be afflicted is to be downcast, depressed, or oppressed.[1] To be restored is to live prosperously and be restored to life or health.[2] God's Word has the power to bring transformation to your thinking, emotions, and your way of life. Martin Luther said, "The soul can do without everything except the word of God, without which none at all of its wants are provided for." God's word is necessary if we desire to walk in God's will for our lives, "And do not be conformed to this world, but be transformed by the renewing of your mind, so that you may prove what the will of God is, that which is good and acceptable and perfect" (Romans 12:2, NAS). Your mind is renewed through the reading, speaking, and ingesting of God's powerful word. Toxic emotions start with toxic thoughts. If you remove "stinking thinking," you will begin to have healed emotions.

Brother Lawrence said, "The most holy and important practice in the spiritual life is the presence of God—that is, every moment to take great pleasure that God is with you" (The Practice of the presence of God). The presence of God is everywhere at all times. The Psalmist wrote, "Where shall I go from your Spirit? Or where shall I flee from your presence? If I ascend to heaven, you are there! If I make my bed in Sheol, you are there!" (Psalm 139:7-8). His Presence is everywhere, but we're not necessarily always aware of Him being near. Max Lucado says, "Don't equate the presence of God with a good mood or a pleasant temperament. God is near whether you are happy or not." His Presence is near, and your hunger for Him will bring a greater awareness of that truth.

David wrote, "You make known to me the path of life; in your presence there is fullness of joy; at your right hand are pleasures forevermore" (Psalm 16:11). The path of life can be found in God's Presence. God's Presence is manifest to us when we hunger for Him (Matthew 5:6). According to Merriam-Webster, to manifest is: to make evident or certain by showing or displaying. God's Presence manifests through joy and peace. Learning to enjoy His Presence establishes us in our faith and creates a culture that's conducive for transformation. I love how the Message Bible reads for 1 Thessalonians 5:23-24, "May God himself, the God who makes everything holy and whole, make you holy and whole, put you together—spirit, soul, and body—and keep you fit for the coming of our Master, Jesus Christ. The One who called you is completely dependable. If he said it, he'll do it!" In His Presence we become holy and whole, and without His Presence we can do nothing of eternal value. Jesus said, "I am the vine; you are the branches. Whoever abides in me and I in him, he it is that bears much fruit, for apart from me you can do nothing" (John 15:5). When we cling to God's Word and His Presence, nothing is impossible.

Nehemiah was able to look upon the ruins with hope because he returned to God and received personal revival and renewal before he came to Jerusalem with a vision for reformation. How can we carry a message of hope and healing without being healed and revived first? Remember, revival begins with me! Nehemiah fasted, prayed, and cried out with a repentant heart for change. He submitted his life to a period of personal reflection, and surrendered to a recalibration for his Nation. His vision became clear through Heaven's cleansing. He was restored and revived so he could become a restorer of that which has been destroyed.

Take time to assess your situation. God has given you a vision for a specific time and strategic moment in history. His desire is to see that vision come to pass in you and through you. It's not just the works around you, but the works within you that He desires to make whole. Invest in His plan by surrendering yourself to the Potter's Wheel. He is the Potter and you are the clay (Isaiah 64:8). He is intricately forming you into precisely what He has designed you to become for the vision He has implanted in your heart.

Action Steps

1. Do you generally run from your problems or face them?
2. Ask someone near and dear, "In your observations, do I run from problems or do I face them?"
3. Take time to assess your situation. What is the motivation of your heart? Are you viewing things through personal pain?
4. What can you do today to confront your problems?
5. Meditate and Journal your thoughts on the following Scripture: "My beloved ones, just like you've always listened to everything I've taught you in the past, I'm asking you now to keep following my instructions as though I were right there with you. Now you must continue to make this new life fully manifested as you live in the holy awe of God—which brings you trembling into his presence. God will continually revitalize you, implanting within you the passion to do what pleases him" (Philippians 2:12-13, TPT).

Notes

1. Strong's H6031.
2. Strong's H2421.

CHAPTER 12

COMMUNICATE THE VISION

"Then I said to them…"

(Nehemiah 2:17a)

"Good leaders must communicate vision clearly, creatively, and continually. However, the vision doesn't come alive until the leader models it."

(John C. Maxwell)

Chrysler Motors was on the brink of failure until they hired a brilliant leader, who brought them from complete irrelevance and near extinction to a thriving and booming corporation. The passionate leader was none other than Lee Iacocca. Lee was born in 1924 to immigrants from Italy, who started their career in America as hotdog vendors. Eventually, Lee's dad borrowed money and became involved in real estate and other ventures, such as owning movie theaters and car-rental companies with a fleet of Ford. Lee became interested in cars due to his father's company.[1]

Lee Iacocca was hired by the Ford Company in 1946 as an engineer, and quickly became a powerful leader within the company. By 1960, he became the Vice President and General Manager of the Ford Company. In 1964, he became known as the "Father of the Mustang." Within two years, the Mustang car brought in $1.1 billion in net profits for the Ford Company. By 1970, Lee was promoted to President of the Ford Company.

Lee became iconic within the company. He was extremely popular with the "who's who" in America and became one of Ford's greatest leaders. The only problem was, his boss, Henry Ford II, despised him. In July of 1978, Lee was fired by Henry Ford II, and other than Ford not liking him, no other reason was given. The Ford Company posted a $1.8 billion profit in 1978, but that wasn't enough for Lee to keep his illustrious position as President of Ford. Several months after being fired, Chrysler Motors hired Lee to rescue their failing company.

Chrysler was riddled with debt and losing millions yearly. Lee took radical measures to bring restoration to a company on the brink of total destruction. He closed down plants and cut the work force down by half, but that wasn't enough. In desperation, he looked to the Federal Government to assist the company with a guaranteed paid back loan. He convinced our Federal Government that Chrysler was much too important to America to allow it to fail. President Jimmy Carter signed a loan guarantee to help Chrysler get back on its feet. Lee assured the President and the Federal Government that he could help Chrysler emerge as a powerful company once again. In 1980, Chrysler lost $1.7 billion. By 1984, Chrysler Motors had a $2.4 billion profit. The company paid back its loan from the Federal Government years before the due date, and Lee Iacocca became the man known for saving a massive motor company from extinction in the United States. His success brought so much notability, many Americans wanted him to run for President of the United States.

Vision has the ability to bring something dead back to life. One of the key proponents to anyone's vision is the ability to communicate clearly what the future could look like. Without the ability to communicate the vision, it will remain dormant. Lee Iacocca said, "You can have brilliant ideas but if you can't get them across, your ideas won't get you anywhere."[2] Lee was a tremendous communicator who was able to express his vision with every company he worked for. The ability to communicate vision inspires others to see what you see. It's not enough for you to see the vision alone, others must hear and see it if they're going to embrace it, and then eventually run with it.

The vision Nehemiah carried was from God, and that vision burned within him. He had four months to ruminate over the Heavenly vision and make it simple and concise for his hearers to understand. It reminds me of the vision God gave the Prophet Habakkuk. Habakkuk was overwhelmed with what he saw, so he began to have conversations with God. This is what the Lord told him, "Write the vision; make it plain on tablets, so he may run who reads it. For still the vision awaits its appointed time; it hastens to the end—it will not lie. If it seems slow, wait for it; it will surely come; it will not delay" (Nehemiah 2:2-3). When the vision is clear to us, we will make it clear to others. I remember the old quote by Cavett Robert, "When it's foggy in the pulpit it's cloudy in the pew." Clarity of vision is imperative for the leader to possess if the vision is going to take flight.

Nehemiah communicated the vision clearly to the one person who mattered the most—the king. Without making his vision clear to the king, the vision would have remained in Nehemiah's heart. Vision that burns within your heart is great, but without that vision burning in others too, progress is stalled. Nehemiah made the vision clear to the king and then received favor to walk the vision out. Once Nehemiah entered Jerusalem, he had to build a team who would see what he saw—Jerusalem safe and prospering. It was critical for him to communicate clearly to his people so they would rise up with him to build the walls. The late CEO of General Electric said, "Without question, communicating the vision has and continues to be, by far, the toughest job we face." Nehemiah mastered this. The proof is in the actions of the people he influenced. What did he say?

Nehemiah said, "You see the trouble we are in, how Jerusalem lies in ruins with its gates burned. Come, let us build the wall of Jerusalem, that we may no longer suffer derision. And I told them of the hand of my God that had been upon me for good, and also of the words that the king had spoken to me" (Nehemiah 2:17-18). Let's break it down:

1. Nehemiah engaged his hearers through sight. "You see the trouble."
2. Nehemiah invited them to take action and build the wall with him. "Come, let us build."
3. Nehemiah urged them to feel. "That we may no longer suffer derision (disgrace)."

4.   Nehemiah assured them. "I told them of the hand of my God that had been upon me for good, and also of the word that the king had spoken to me."

Nehemiah was engaging, inviting, urgent, and assuring. It's not just what he said, but how he communicated what was in his heart. He communicated his vision with great passion coupled with immense hope. He was saying, "C'mon everyone, we can do this! We all know this place is a mess, but we have the favor of God and the king upon us, to repair and restore this wall for our generation and the generations to come! No more disgrace! Time to restore our dignity as God's People." How did the people respond? "And they said, 'Let us rise up and build'" (Nehemiah 2:18). That's powerful! Robert T. Kiyosaki says, "True passion attracts. If you have passion in your business, the right people will be attracted to your team." Nehemiah attracted a Dream Team.

What was once burning in one man's soul was now burning in many-a-man's soul. Vision is contagious! Vision communicated with passion and hope will set others on fire for God's plan and purpose. What started with a spark inside one person became a fire amongst the masses. Christi's grandfather, Otto Voegele, was driving on Highway 200 near Zap, ND, when his tire blew up. Otto decided to drive his vehicle a couple more miles with the tire blown and the rim rubbing along the hot black asphalt. You know where this story is going? The rim produced sparks and the sparks flew into the dry hot ditch. What started with a spark became a ditch on fire. Do you know what happens when a dry hot ditch catches on fire? It spreads! It's amazing what one spark can do. Nehemiah's communication was the spark that lit the fire!

Nehemiah had to feel excited when he wrote, "So they strengthened their hands for the good work" (Nehemiah 2:18). Nehemiah had prepared himself for months. By this time, he was probably like a horse in a stall at the starting gate of a race. When he heard, "Let us rise and build," it was probably the sweetest five words he'd ever heard. His preparation time certainly wasn't wasted time. The times of listening, prayer, fasting, repenting, waiting, and then boldly stepping forward in faith, was now paying off. The team was engaged and ready to build. Nehemiah had successfully become a leader amongst his people. John Maxwell says, "Leadership is influence." Nehemiah started a reformation and led it successfully to completion.

Communicating a vision is much more than words. You've heard it said, "A picture is worth a thousand words." The same is true when communicating vision. For the last fifteen years, I've been hearing in my spirit, "Paint a picture. Paint a picture." I know exactly what that means. If I'm going to effectively communicate our vision for planting multiple churches, mobilizing people in missions around the world, and equipping future leaders, I must paint a picture that communicates our future. How do you do that? In 2009, our church hosted a conference with a special guest speaker who spoke in the evenings, while I spoke in one of the afternoon sessions. We invited people to come with their canvases to paint a picture as I was sharing my vision for our church, city, and region. I spoke, they painted. This is just one way to "paint a picture"—literally do it. When people see it with their own eyes, they begin to grab hold of the vision and take ownership of it. They begin to ask, "What is my part in this vision? How can I use my God-given gifts to help accomplish the vision?" Vision is contagious if communicated clearly.

Another practical way of "painting a picture" is through word pictures. Our Aberdeen Freedom Church is known as "the Hub inside The Hub." Our city is known as "The Hub City." During a twenty-eight day fast in 2004, I heard this, "Hub inside The Hub." With those words in my spirit came a picture of a wheel with spokes stretching out to other towns in our region. I began to hear the words and see a picture of our future. These words and pictures in my spirit changed the course of my life forever. I kept those words near and dear to me for six months. The only other person I shared them with was my wife. Six months later, she went on a twenty-one day fast. At the end of the fast, we were ministering in North Dakota when a friend of ours stood behind a microphone and literally said, "Drew and Christi, I know you live in Aberdeen and it's called 'The Hub City,' but Drew and Christi, you are the 'Hub inside The Hub.'" I looked at Christi and said, "I told you." From that moment, we began to run with the vision. Pictures paint a thousand words!

The best way to "paint a picture" is by becoming the picture. You must model it. If you want others to "buy into it," you as the leader must set an example every day. One of John Maxwell's most famous quotes is, "A leader is one who knows the way, goes the way, and shows the way." Nehemiah was that leader. He knew the direction of the Lord, he had a strategy to fulfill the vision, and he put his hands to work with all the people. Nehemiah didn't remain in the king's palace in Susa, barking orders from a thousand miles away, while the people labored feverishly everyday to complete the "man of God's" vision. Nehemiah made the trip to Jerusalem and became the picture. You can't lead others where you aren't willing to go. If I advise someone to live by faith in a certain area of their life, I better be leading the way in that area.

Here's another old saying, "Actions speak louder than words." I think it's safe to say that this age-old maxim was drawn from the well of Scripture. James, inspired by Holy Spirit, wrote, "So also faith, if it does not have works (deeds and actions of obedience to back it up), by itself is destitute of power (inoperative, dead)" (James 2:17, AMPC). You can shout the vision out on the mountain tops, but if you don't take steps toward the vision, it's useless, powerless. Thomas Edison once said, "Vision without execution is hallucination." Dream a dream, but for heaven's sake, take action!

Myles Munroe said, "People generally fall into one of three groups: the few who make things happen, the many who watch things happen, and the overwhelming majority who have no notion of what happens. Every person is either a creator of fact or a creature of circumstance. He either puts color into his environment, or, like a chameleon, takes color from his environment."[3] I think during different seasons of our life, all of us have either visited or lived habitually in one of the categories mentioned by Myles. Eventually, if we're going to see the vision come to fruition, we must communicate to the people we're leading by our actions. It's crucial we become the few who make things happen. James also penned, "But be doers of the word, and not hearers only, deceiving yourselves" (James 1:22). Holy Spirit, through James, was and is challenging all Believers in Christ to read God's Word, trust God's Word, and act upon God's Word. The same is true about vision. When God gives us His vision for our lives on Earth, it's our responsibility to be good stewards of that vision. To be a good steward of vision is to fully embrace it and receive personal responsibility for your part in fulfilling it. Don't deceive yourself. Without action, your vision is dead.

To be a great visionary leader, clear and concise communication is inescapable. Like Nehemiah, we must engage, invite, urge, and assure the people we're leading. Nehemiah became a messenger of hope by "painting a picture" through his words, through using the conditions around him, and ultimately through his actions. The vision is too important for us to be lazy in our efforts of communicating a future that God wants us to possess. If we ask, God will grant us the ability to communicate His heart. Through anointed communication, what lies dormant will come to life, the ruins will be restored, and the impossible will become possible. You can do it! You can lead effectively and powerfully! It's time to run with the vision!

Action Steps

1. Write down your vision in your journal.
2. Break it down into one paragraph.
3. Paint a picture with your words. Use metaphors to describe your vision. Express your vision through illustrations.
4. Literally paint a picture or have someone paint a picture that expresses your vision.
5. Meditate and Journal your thoughts on the following Scripture: "Write the vision; make it plain on tablets, so he may run who reads it" (Habakkuk 2:2).

Notes

1. Jacey Fortin contributed reporting. A version of this article appears in print on July 4, 2019, Section B, Page 16 of the New York edition with the headline: "Lee Iacocca, Who Got Ford and Chrysler Humming, Is Dead at 94."
2. Asad Meah, "35 Inspirational Lee Iacocca Quotes On Success," *Awaken the Greatness Within*, (May 19, 2018). https://www.awakenthegreatnesswithin.com/35-inspirational-lee-iacocca-quotes-on-success/.
3. Myles Munroe, *Understanding Your Potential: Discovering the Hidden You*. (Shippensburg: Destiny Image, Inc.), 2011.

CHAPTER 13

ALL HANDS ON DECK!

"So they strengthened their hands for the good work."

(Nehemiah 2:18b)

"Teamwork is the ability to work together toward a common vision. The
ability to direct individual accomplishments toward organizational objectives.
It is the fuel that allows common people to attain uncommon results."

(Andrew Carnegie)

It was a normal Tuesday morning in September. I woke up early, read the
Word, prayed, and was probably thinking about calling my sister on her birthday. Little did I know, everything in our world was about to change. It was
September 11, 2001, which we now refer to as 9/11. My mother-in-law, Linda,
called around 9:00 a.m., "Drew, have you been watching the news?" I recognized an urgency in her voice and immediately knew something was terribly
wrong. We didn't have access to news stations on our TV, and smart phones
weren't in existence at the time. I was clueless. Linda began to describe in utter
shock and disbelief what she was watching on her television as the first tower
was burning after it had been struck by the first plane. I quickly got in my car
and drove to my in-law's house to view and hear what was happening in New
York City.

By the time I got to their house, a second plane had flown into the other tower. Shortly after, we heard two other planes were hijacked. American Airlines

flight 77 hit the Pentagon and United Airlines flight 93 crashed eighty miles southeast of Pittsburgh, near a town called Shanksville, PA. From 8:45 a.m. to 10:37 a.m., in less than two hours, our country experienced terrorism on our soil like we've never seen before. It was different because it was an attack on the Continental U.S. and was visible to all of us through the mainstream media. The pictures and videos of the planes hitting the towers, people jumping or being catapulted to their deaths, the towers collapsing, smoke and debris consuming the city, people running, people bleeding, and the look of terror on their faces will forever be etched in my mind. The managing editor of Time magazine wrote on that day, "Terrorism has struck America before, but never this brazenly and never with such heartbreaking destruction."[1] It truly was one of the saddest days our country has ever encountered.

President George W. Bush addressed our Nation at 8:30 p.m., September 11, from the Oval Office. His message was powerful and is worth repeating:

> "Today, our fellow citizens, our way of life, our very freedom came under attack in a series of deliberate and deadly terrorist acts. The victims were in airplanes or in their offices—secretaries, businessmen and women, military and federal workers. Moms and dads. Friends and neighbors.
>
> Thousands of lives were suddenly ended by evil, despicable acts of terror. The pictures of airplanes flying into buildings, fires burning, huge structures collapsing, have filled us with disbelief, terrible sadness and a quiet, unyielding anger.
>
> These acts of mass murder were intended to frighten our nation into chaos and retreat. But they have failed. Our country is strong. A great people has been moved to defend a great nation.
>
> Terrorist attacks can shake the foundations of our biggest buildings, but they cannot touch the foundation of America. These acts shatter steel, but they cannot dent the steel of American resolve.

America was targeted for attack because we're the brightest beacon for freedom and opportunity in the world. And no one will keep that light from shining. Today, our nation saw evil, the very worst of human nature, and we responded with the best of America, with the daring of our rescue workers, with the caring for strangers and neighbors who came to give blood and help in any way they could.

Immediately following the first attack, I implemented our government's emergency response plans. Our military is powerful, and it's prepared. Our emergency teams are working in New York City and Washington, D.C., to help with local rescue efforts.

Our first priority is to get help to those who have been injured and to take every precaution to protect our citizens at home and around the world from further attacks.

The functions of our government continue without interruption. Federal agencies in Washington which had to be evacuated today are reopening for essential personnel tonight and will be open for business tomorrow.

Our financial institutions remain strong, and the American economy will be open for business as well.

The search is underway for those who are behind these evil acts. I've directed the full resources for our intelligence and law enforcement communities to find those responsible and bring them to justice. We will make no distinction between the terrorists who committed these acts and those who harbor them.

I appreciate so very much the members of Congress who have joined me in strongly condemning these attacks. And on behalf of the American people, I thank the many world leaders who have called to offer their condolences and assistance.

America and our friends and allies join with all those who want peace and security in the world and we stand together to win the war against terrorism.

Tonight I ask for your prayers for all those who grieve, for the children whose worlds have been shattered, for all whose sense of safety and security has been threatened. And I pray they will be comforted by a power greater than any of us spoken through the ages in Psalm 23: 'Even though I walk through the valley of the shadow of death, I fear no evil, for You are with me.'

This is a day when all Americans from every walk of life unite in our resolve for justice and peace. America has stood down enemies before, and we will do so this time.

None of us will ever forget this day, yet we go forward to defend freedom and all that is good and just in our world.

Thank you. Good night and God bless America."[2]

President Bush spoke words of comfort to the broken. He was also sending a message to our enemy that we will not be retreating, but fighting back on behalf of justice and the security of our Nation. His message called us to pray and unify under the banners of peace, justice, and freedom. He called us to arise and take action. The old Naval cry is, "All Hands on Deck!" All Hands mean, "Everyone on board this ship, pay attention! We need everyone's help because we are in a crisis situation." Our President's speech struck a nerve in millions of Americans and we became united as a force to bring justice and restoration to our Country.

Our first responders didn't need a battle cry that day. It was just their duty to respond to emergency situations. They were "All Hands on Deck" on September 11th. Police officers, firemen, EMT's, and a multitude of other people were there to help and rescue people from the destruction and debris. The death toll amongst firefighters and police workers was over four hundred.[3] Our entire Country watched their valiant efforts, which inspired all of us to arise and unite for a greater cause.

Nehemiah had a cause! He had a vision that was burning within him. He communicated effectively and the proof is in chapter three of the Book of Nehemiah. The people saw the vision, felt the urgency, and "they strengthened their hands for the good work" (Nehemiah 2:18b). When God's People rise together as one, all things are possible. Andrew Carnegie said, "Teamwork is the fuel that allows common people to attain uncommon results." Steve Jobs said, "Great things in business are never done by one person; they're done by a team of people." Nehemiah was empowered by God to inspire people to accomplish something that was beyond themselves. If you have a vision from God, it will always include other people to assist you in finishing the work.

"Lone Rangers" are becoming strangers. Author John Hatcher says, "Our American culture paints a picture of masculinity where a man is an island. A lone cowboy on the prairie smoking Marlboros. A caped crusader who works better alone. A dad in his den, reading the paper, shooing the kids away so he can unwind. But this lone ranger mentality is dangerous. Even the actual Lone Ranger had Tonto. We're not made to be alone." I think "Lone Rangers" were celebrated more in our Country's past. The younger generation is embracing a team model in churches, sports, and many other professions.

John Maxwell says, "Teamwork makes the dream work." In years past, most churches had one primary communicator—the Lead Pastor. Now, churches are adopting a team of communicators throughout the year. There may be one that communicates more than the rest, but leaders now understand that having a team is more effective because different anointings impact different people in a variety of ways. I can communicate a truth for three weeks straight, then have someone else communicate the same truth in a different way and some people are in awe, saying, "Wow, that was a great word!" I may have communicated the exact same thing, but they heard it a different way and it finally registered. There was a time that would have extremely frustrated me, now I rejoice because the hearer hears.

Chapter three of Nehemiah records the people who worked on the wall. The list includes many names which I'll leave out, but here's a list of the various types of people who helped Nehemiah build:

1. Priests.
2. Goldsmiths.
3. Perfumers.
4. Temple Servants.
5. Merchants.
6. Sons of Rulers of Districts.

I don't mention names because the point of chapter three is not to give credit to every person who put their hands to work, but to express to the reader that teamwork is necessary to accomplish God's dream for us on Earth. Harry Truman said, "It is amazing what you can accomplish if you do not care who gets the credit." I don't think any of these people wanted credit as much as they wanted to simply do the right thing. They were committed to restoring Jerusalem and their dignity. It was a God-given vision that brought purpose to one generation and hope to the next. The former chairman and CEO of Starbucks, Howard Schultz, said, "Success is best when it's shared." People working together to see the vision accomplished is the message of Nehemiah chapter three. A message we need to hear and live by in our generation.

What do you do when people don't "run with the vision" with you? I think it's important for us as leaders to evaluate how we're communicating the vision and ask people, "Am I communicating the vision clearly?" I've noticed too, that when we communicate the vision, steps must be taken towards the vision so momentum builds and people can see and experience the progress. It's not enough to "blow the trumpet" but never take action. Once again, "Actions speak louder than words." Saying all of that, some people will continue to not put their hands to the work.

In Nehemiah chapter three, only one group of people wouldn't work—the nobles within the Tekoite clan. The "normal class" people amongst the Tekoites worked, but their "wealthy class" "would not stoop to serve their Lord" (Nehemiah 3:5b). They wouldn't get their hands dirty for the cause of the Kingdom. Their lack of fervency and cooperation didn't stop Nehemiah for one second, nor did others lack in fervency. In fact, the "normal class" of the Tekoites worked harder. "Then came the people of Tekoa, who repaired another section across from the great projecting tower and over to the wall of Ophel" (Nehemiah 3:27). They did double duty. I wonder if they did double duty because they lacked support from the "elite squad"? Some call it the "20/80 rule," which is 20 percent of the people doing 80 percent of the work. Or, maybe the Tekoites worked with a fervent spirit because they were running with the vision and had the passion to finish and finish strong. The bottom line is, when others don't put their hands to the good work, don't stop!

When a group of people work together for a Kingdom cause, God shows up and empowers that people to complete the task! The power of unity and perseverance is a key ingredient to completing the God-given vision. Stephen Covey says, "Interdependent people combine their own effort with the efforts of others to achieve their greatest success." That's what Nehemiah and the good people did when they combined their gift sets and put their hands to work on restoring the wall. Our Country did the same on, and after, September 11. The call of our time is, "All Hands on Deck!" We have a vision to fulfill and work to finish. Though some don't run with us, we know God is for us, and is empowering us to finish strong!

Action Steps

1.   On a scale from 1 to 10, how do you rate yourself as a team player?
2.   What are three steps you can take immediately to become a better team player? Write them down in your journal and act immediately.
3.   Ask others you work with, "How can I be a better team player?" Decide in your heart that you won't become defensive when they answer you honestly. Listen to them and then write down their answers.

4. Create a strategy for the team you lead on how to create a culture of honor, community, and teamwork.

5. Meditate and Journal your thoughts on the following Scripture: "Every believer has received grace gifts, so use them to serve one another as faithful stewards of the many-colored tapestry of God's grace. For example, if you have a speaking gift, speak as though God were speaking his words through you.[a] If you have the gift of serving, do it passionately with the strength God gives you,[b] so that in everything God alone will be glorified through Jesus Christ. For to him belong the power and the glory forever throughout all ages! Amen" (1 Peter 4:10-12, TPT).

Notes

1. James Kelly, "To Our Readers," *Time Magazine*, September 11, 2001.
2. George W. Bush, "Text of Bush's Address," *Cable News Network*, 2001.
3. Peter L. Bergen, "September 11 attacks," *Encyclopedia Britannica*, 2001.

CHAPTER 14

A MIND TO WORK

"So we built the wall. And all the wall was joined together to half its height, for the people had a mind to work."

(Nehemiah 4:6)

"The biggest wall you have to climb is the one you build in your mind: never let your mind talk you out of your dreams, trick you into giving up. Never let your mind become the greatest obstacle to success. To get your mind on the right track, the rest will follow."

(Roy T. Bennett in *The Light in the Heart*)[1]

Orville and Wilbur Wright go down in our history books as American Aviators who invented, built, and flew the first airplane. Like any other world-changing discovery, they had many obstacles facing them. One of these obstacles was the doubters. Many people criticized their efforts and communicated their aversion toward the Wright Brothers and other inventors who attempted to build something they thought was impossible.

Here are a few of the opinions during that era of discovery:

"Is it not demonstrated that a true flying machine, self-raising, self-sustaining, self-propelling, is physically impossible?" (Joseph LeConte, November 1888").

"It is apparent to me that the possibilities of the aeroplane, which two or three years ago were thought to hold the solution to the [flying machine] problem, have been exhausted, and that we must turn elsewhere" (Thomas Edison, November 1895).

"I can state flatly that heavier than air flying machines are impossible" (Lord Kelvin, 1895).

"I have not the smallest molecule of faith in aerial navigation other than ballooning, or of the expectation of good results from any of the trials we heard of. So you will understand that I would not care to be a member of the Aeronautical Society" (Lord Kelvin, 1896).

"It is complete nonsense to believe flying machines will ever work" (Stanley Mosley, 1905).

"The aeroplane will never fly" (Lord Haldane, 1907).

Some of the most influential people during this age of discovery believed man would never fly in the sky. Their doubts and criticisms served the Wright Brothers as fuel for their project rather than interference. Needless to say, the Wright Brothers began to soar with their vision to fly. Richard Bach said, "Argue for your limitations and, sure enough, they're yours." The Wright Brothers saw "the sky as their limit," while others were bound to the dirt under their feet.

The Apostle Paul, inspired by God, wrote, "Stop imitating the ideals and opinions of the culture around you, but be inwardly transformed by the Holy Spirit through a total reformation of how you think. This will empower you to discern God's will as you live a beautiful life, satisfying and perfect in his eyes" (Romans 12:2, TPT). The word "transformed" comes from a Greek word, "metamorphoō."[2] We draw the word "metamorphose" from this Greek word. The picture is a caterpillar in the cocoon. Before the caterpillar becomes the butterfly, it's transformed in the cocoon. The caterpillar becomes a liquid substance, and then forms wings. What was once bound to the ground can take flight because of the transformation.

Our minds are the same—they need transformation. When Jesus commanded people to "repent," He wasn't just talking about people becoming sorrowful for their actions, He was telling them to change their thinking. One of the greatest obstacles we face is not external, but internal. Laird Hamilton said, "Make sure your worst enemy doesn't live between your own two ears." Our minds are a battlefield, and it behooves us to recognize the war that's being waged over our thinking. If we think wrong thoughts, our actions will eventually follow. Thoughts affect emotions, and emotions can impact our actions in a positive or negative fashion. In her bestselling book, *Battlefield of the Mind*, Joyce Meyer writes, "The mind is the leader or forerunner of all actions."[3]

The Apostle Paul recognized the battle over our minds when he wrote:

> For although we live in the natural realm, we don't wage a military campaign employing human weapons, using manipulation to achieve our aims. Instead, our spiritual weapons are energized with divine power to effectively dismantle the defenses behind which people hide. We can demolish every deceptive fantasy that opposes God and break through every arrogant attitude that is raised up in defiance of the true knowledge of God. We capture, like prisoners of war, every thought and insist that it bow in obedience to the Anointed One.
>
> (2 Corinthians 10:3-5, TPT)

What are those weapons of warfare that empower us in this battle over the mind? Paul lists them in Ephesians 6 as: the Word of God, Prayer, our Righteousness in Christ (new identity), Faith, Peace, and our union with Christ through Salvation. One of my all-time favorite books is *The Three Battlegrounds* by Francis Frangipane. He writes, "You will remember that the location where Jesus was crucified was called 'Golgotha,' which meant 'place of the skull.' If we will be effective in spiritual warfare, the first field of conflict where we must learn warfare is the battleground of the mind; i.e., the 'place of the skull.' Indeed, the territory of the un-crucified thought-life is the beachhead of satanic assault in our lives. To defeat the devil, we must be renewed in the spirit of our minds."[4] If we stay strong in the Lord by stewarding our thoughts, we will complete the vision He has assigned to us for this planet in our lifetime.

Nehemiah and the good people laboring with him "had a mind to work." They were relentless to start the work on the wall and resolute to finish it. Did they have opposition? The nobles of that region, Sanballat and Tobiah, were furious. They didn't want to see the Jews prosper. They sent threats of impending destruction and attempted to strike fear in Nehemiah and his team. Nehemiah refused to quit! He was bold, courageous, and unflinching. He set his heart and mind on God's plan rather than the enemies' threats. His enemies were attempting to strike fear in his mind so he would retreat and stop the good work. His mind was set, and he wasn't going to back down! No compromise!

Rather than shrinking back in fear, Nehemiah devised a new plan—an effective strategy to combat the possibility of any of their enemies overcoming them. Sometimes we just need to shift our thinking to finish the vision God has given us. The vision never changes, but the strategy which we use may alter. Nehemiah had half of the men working on construction and half of them holding weapons to fight off any ensuing enemies. Some had a weapon in one hand while they were building the wall with the other. They were prepared! They were set for action! They weren't going to abandon the project because of threats and accusations. Nehemiah was forced to change his approach to finishing the project, but wouldn't allow opposition to stop him from building.

Making progress with our vision can be exhilarating. Celebrate every victory! Focus on what has been accomplished thus far and the lives you have impacted. You'll have plenty of setbacks and difficulties on your journey, but don't allow the obstacles to dwarf the breakthroughs. We have a tendency to make mountains out of molehills. God has a tendency to look at mountains and reduce them to nothing. He invites us to do the same. When God spoke to Zerubbabel about finishing the Temple, He said, "This is the word of the Lord to Zerubbabel: 'Not by might, nor by power, but by my Spirit,' says the Lord of hosts. 'Who are you, O great mountain? Before Zerubbabel you shall become a plain. And he shall bring forward the top stone amid shouts of "Grace, grace to it!"'" (Zechariah 4:6-7). Our mountains become nothing in God's Presence. During times of pressure, draw near to God and watch His Mighty Hand move!

If God gave this vision to you, don't you think He'll also accomplish it through you? God isn't about playing games with us. He doesn't keep the proverbial "golden carrot" before our eyes to simply frustrate us. God is for us and He wants the vision to be carried out! God also said to Zerubbabel, "The hands of Zerubbabel have laid the foundation of this temple; his hands will also complete it. Then you will know that the Lord Almighty has sent me to you" (Zechariah 4:8). God doesn't leave us in the middle of our quest to fulfill the vision. He is good and He delights in our victories. The Prophet Nahum proclaimed, "The Lord is good, a refuge in times of trouble. He cares for those who trust in him" (Nahum 1:7). He is a Good God and is our refuge in difficult times. The only thing He wants from us is our trust. Will we trust Him? God's pattern, recorded in multiple places in Scripture, is to finish what He starts. We sometimes think that God is only good some of the time and not all the time. Or, we think God will do it for others but not for us. I read somewhere, "God is no respecter of persons" (Acts 10:34). He is for you!

If any of our thoughts are in contradiction to the Lord being good, we have believed a lie. Several years ago, I began to envision what I thought God wanted for our ministry in Beulah, ND. Outpourings were happening in Toronto, Smithton, MO, and Pensacola, Florida. Each of these Revivals had similar attributes—a few particular preachers God was moving through. I envisioned the same happening in Beulah. We had a guest Evangelist coming to Beulah and he was anointed. Our ministry team was prepared to host extended meetings if necessary. My expectations of an outpouring like Pensacola had reached an all-time high. I was sure this was our appointed time.

The night before our guest was scheduled to fly in, our Lead Pastor received a phone call from another pastor in our region. The pastor communicated some of his concerns about our guest evangelist. Our Lead Pastor contacted me after his conversation and asked me to come to his house. It was about 9:00 p.m., so I knew something was brewing. After discussing the concerns of the other pastor, we thought it was necessary for us to contact the Evangelist. It was about 9:30 p.m. our time and 11:30 p.m. his time. The Evangelist answered the phone and our Lead Pastor asked him about the concerns that had been presented to us through the pastor. The Evangelist said, "I will call you in the morning. I'm in a hotel room with my family right now and I don't want to wake them up." The next morning came and went and we never heard from him. In fact, that was 1996 and he hasn't called back yet. Maybe that morning will never come.

After months of prayer and preparation, I felt like the wind was knocked out of me. I was grieving over the possible condition of the Evangelist and I was mourning over what I thought was supposed to happen in our church. Several weeks went by and I remained in a place of confusion. One night at a corporate prayer meeting, I began to weep. I couldn't stop. It was one of those moments in time where the cries would not be contained. Bobby Conner calls it, "Ballin' and Squallin'." That's the Southern version of what was transpiring in that special moment.

Everyone left the building and I remained in God's manifest Presence. I knew He was about to speak to my heart. As I listened to Him speak, I heard the following, "Drew, I am removing the 'dis' from your life." I thought, "What is the 'dis'?" I went to my office and looked up the word "dis" in my dictionary. Do you know what I read? Here is one of Merriam-Webster's definitions: the Roman god of the underworld. When used as a prefix, it means the opposite of something: disrespect, disunity, distract, disorder, disrupt, discourage, and disappoint. After I read the definition, it began to make sense to me. God is opposite of all the words I mentioned above. "Dis—the Roman god of the underworld" makes sense too. What I heard next rocked my world, "Drew, I am going to erase dis-appointment with my appointment!" Wow! I stood in awe of God's beautiful voice. I continue to learn a valuable lesson throughout my life—if I can trust His heart, I will trust His Hand. God's character never changes, but the way He moves, does.

The significance of hearing His voice is multi-faceted. Where this particular occurrence in my life was concerned, hearing His voice erased disappointment and brought great hope for a wonderful future. Had this disappointment continued, I'm confident a stronghold of lies would have crystallized in my soul. One lie feeds another lie and creates a fortress that repels truth. Our views of God become skewed by our unhealed pain. Lies become the strongholds in our minds, and the only way these lies come tumbling down is through revelation of the truth. Jesus was speaking to Jews who believed Him when He said,

"If you abide in my word, you are truly my disciples, and you will know the truth, and the truth will set you free" (John 8:31-32). Abide in Jesus' words, become His disciple, know the truth, and you will be free.

The foundation of true freedom is Jesus. When we build upon this foundation, it's imperative we build with the revelation of His Word. The Psalmist said, "Your word is a lamp to my feet and a light to my path" (Psalm 119:105). Light speaks of revelation. The "lamp to my feet" speaks to us of today, and "light to my path" speaks to us of our future. God's Word brings light and expels the darkness in our minds. True transformation can only become attainable when we discipline ourselves in reading, speaking, and meditating on God's Word.

It's not enough to wipe the hard drive. Some think meditation is simply getting everything out of our minds that troubles our soul. Biblical meditation is viewing God's Word and declaring it continuously. It's almost like a cow chewing on its cud. Cows have to chew repeatedly in order to digest their food correctly. Cows chew about eight hours a day, as stated by Cattle-empire.net. When we chew on God's Word, our minds will begin to be flooded with revelation, setting us free from the lies that attempt to impede our spiritual growth and progress in completing the Heavenly vision.

The late great evangelist, Smith Wigglesworth, said, "There are four principles we need to maintain: first, read the Word of God. Second, consume the Word of God until it consumes you. Third, believe the Word of God. Fourth, act on the Word." As essential as meditation is to fulfilling the Heavenly vision, action is what separates the good and the great. The Apostle James wrote, "But be doers of the word, and not hearers only, deceiving yourselves" (James 1:22). Read, speak, meditate, believe, and then take action!

Nehemiah had the truth branded in his mind. When accusations and lies were hurled toward him, he responded with truth, "Do not be afraid of them. Remember the Lord, who is great and awesome, and fight for your brothers, your sons, your daughters, your wives, and your homes" (Nehemiah 4:14). He wouldn't permit the threats to dominate his thoughts or his actions. He cast down fear and reminded himself and his team to look upon the One who is "great and awesome." Nehemiah fought "the good fight of faith," knowing the fight wasn't just about himself, but for all of Jerusalem and the sake of their posterity.

Action Steps

1. Take time to think about what you've been thinking about. What dominates your thinking? Journal the thoughts that occupy your mind.
2. Are your dominating thoughts constructive or destructive? Are your thoughts more negative or positive?
3. How will you change your thought life from negative to positive? Write down a daily strategy that you can implement to renew your mind.
4. Find Scriptures to combat lies you have believed. Write them down and declare them daily.
5. Meditate and Journal your thoughts on the following Scripture: "This Book of the Law shall not depart from your mouth, but you shall meditate on it day and night, so that you may be careful to do according to all that is written in it. For then you will make your way prosperous, and then you will have good success" (Joshua 1:8).

Notes

1. Roy T. Bennett, *The Light in the Heart*. (Roy T. Bennett, 2020).
2. Strong's G3339.
3. Joyce Meyer, *Battlefield of the mind: Winning the Battle in Your Mind*. (New York: FaithWords, 2017), 11.
4. Francis Frangipane, *The Three Battlegrounds*. (Cedar Rapids, IA: Arrow Publications, 2006), 1.

CHAPTER 15

LEAVING A LEGACY

"Do not be afraid of them. Remember the Lord, who is great and awesome, and fight for your brothers, your sons, your daughters, your wives, and your homes."

(Nehemiah 4:14)

"All good men and women must take responsibility to create legacies that will take the next generation to a level we could only imagine."

(Jim Rohn)

It was the spring of 2005 and I was walking the streets of Vienna, Austria. I had finished a week of preaching the Gospel in Romania, and Vienna was our last stop before we flew back to the States. Romania was my second ever overseas missions' trip. Just three years prior to that, I heard the call of God to go to the Nations and preach. It was surreal because growing up in Aberdeen, SD, I was a shy boy who never dreamt of going beyond the borders of the United States. If you'd have told me during my freshman year of college, "Drew, someday you're going to preach and go to the Nations," I would've laughed at you and told you emphatically, "You are crazy!" I avoided some majors in college because I became aware that I would be required to take a speech class. Yikes!

As we were walking throughout Vienna, our guide (a regional director of missions), stopped and said, "Drew, do you see that cathedral in the distance? The people that started the construction and laid the foundation of the cathedral knew they would never see the end product." That moment has been etched in my mind and spirit since 2005. I began to imagine our vision coming to life. I began to dream of the churches we would start and how these churches would impact regions. I began to preach on legacy and how our commitment to the Heavenly vision would impact generations. One of my favorite lines became, "This is not about you and I here, today. This vision is about the generations to come!" My favorite verse became Isaiah 44:3-4, "For I will pour water on him who is thirsty, and floods on the dry ground; I will pour My Spirit on your descendants, and My blessing on your offspring; they will spring up among the grass like willows by the watercourses." Our thirst for God not only blesses one generation, but the generations to come! That was my message in 2005 and that continues to be my message. The decisions we make today set a precedence for the generations to come.

Bill Johnson says, "Another generation's 'ceiling' in God can become our spiritual 'floor.'" In other words, what I become and accomplish through God's power in my lifetime is only a starting point for my children—a place for them to stand on. My parents paved a way for me. In 1979, they surrendered to Jesus Christ. They became believers and followers of Jesus. I'm eternally grateful to my Grandma Becker for praying fervently for us, and Pastor Robert James for reaching out to my parents and leading them to Christ. Through their following of Jesus and leading me in my younger years, I also became a follower of Jesus. I may have taken a few detours on the path, but I returned with a blaze of glory.

Billy Graham said, "The greatest legacy one can pass on to one's children and grandchildren is not money or other material things accumulated in one's life, but rather a legacy of character and faith." The walls Nehemiah and his team built were more than an external sign of prosperity, but an internal work of God to restore and rebuild a Nation's hope and dignity. Nehemiah's faith was contagious. He led the people as he was led by God. His commitment to persist through persecution became the foundation for a reformation amongst his people.

What motivated this man of God to finish the race? He began the race with a question and would finish with an exclamation point. What got him through?

Maybe a better question would be, "Who got him through?" The answer is in Nehemiah 4:14, "Remember the Lord, who is great and awesome, and fight for your brothers, your sons, your daughters, your wives, and your homes." The Lord, and the people he was fighting for, gave Nehemiah the courage to finish. Ultimately, the vision God has imparted into you isn't just for you, but for the many people you will impact by finishing the work God has entrusted to you.

Some of the greatest heroes of our time will be the ones who are able to keep their eyes on the eternal rewards, rather than the temporal sacrifices. Exhorting Believers, Paul writes, "...looking to Jesus, the founder and perfecter of our faith, who for the joy that was set before him endured the cross, despising the shame, and is seated at the right hand of the throne of God" (Hebrews 12:2). Jesus endured the shame of the Cross because He was able to see the eternal purpose beyond the temporal pain. His joy came from His view of eternity. His joy to become the ultimate and exclusive sacrifice for all humanity, far outweighed the pain and the shame.

Vision in action is about a process by which we submit ourselves to a living God who has a plan and purpose for our lives. The vision you carry is never about yourself. At times in this process, you will want to quit. The pressure and pain may feel greater than what you could ever endure. These are the moments and seasons of decision. It's in these valleys we become resolute and determined to finish, or discouraged and disillusioned in our pain. In 1991, I experienced one of these deep valleys. Rather than quitting, I decided to seek God with my entire being. God's Word, His manifest Presence, and other Believers in Christ, sustained me in the valley. The thought of my future, having a family, and my young cousins in Seattle, compelled me to never give up.

What I couldn't see in 1991, I cherish now. I've been married for twenty-two years to a beautiful and loving wife, Christi. We have four amazing children who bless us every day. Through God's strength, we have preached overseas in Africa, China, Ukraine, and Romania. We have started two churches with the greatest people on the planet. In 2019, we started a childcare center we call, "Just Kidding Childcare Center." We've seen hundreds of people saved, baptized, and discipled. Lives have been changed eternally and our rewards await us in Heaven. None of this would've been a reality if I had given up in 1991. Peter Senge says, "It's not what the vision is, it's what the vision does." The vision has changed my life and direction, and has impacted the lives of many others. Our present pain is tolerable when we embrace an eternal perspective.

The Scriptures are filled with stories of men and women who fought against all odds to accomplish the Heavenly vision in their generation and leave a legacy in the next. Noah found favor with God and was asked by God to build an ark. "A what?" Noah could have replied. Noah had no grid for what God was talking about. No human had ever seen an ark. In fact, no human had experienced rain falling, and now God was saying it's going to pour for forty days and forty nights! Honestly, that would've sounded crazy to me. Scripture says, "By faith Noah, being warned by God concerning events as yet unseen, in reverent fear constructed an ark for the saving of his household" (Hebrews 11:7a). Noah revered God, obeyed the Heavenly vision, and saved his lineage from complete destruction. Oh yeah, it took him a hundred and twenty years to complete it.

Abram was called by God to go to a land he had no knowledge of and serve God Almighty, who his family had never recognized. God changed his name to Abraham and promised him to be the Father of many Nations. That could have sounded ludicrous to Abraham at the time, considering he had no children. His wife, Sarah, conceived Isaac at the young age of ninety, yet, the Heavenly vision became a reality. Scripture says:

> And Abraham's faith did not weaken, even though, at about 100 years of age, he figured his body was as good as dead— and so was Sarah's womb. Abraham never wavered in believing God's promise. In fact, his faith grew stronger, and in this he brought glory to God. He was fully convinced that God is able to do whatever he promises.
>
> (Romans 4:19-21)

Abraham's faith did not weaken. He believed in God's plan for his life and left a legacy! You can hardly say his name without saying, "Abraham, Isaac, and Jacob." God's perspective is generational because He is "the Alpha and Omega." He is eternal. God sees the beginning and the end. He fashions every generation after His eternal perspective.

Joseph was the son of Jacob. He was the dreamer boy who wore the coat of many colors. God gave Joseph night visions of his destiny as a great leader amongst his brothers and fellow man. Through jealousy and hatred, Joseph's brothers threw him in a pit and sold him into slavery. He went from the pit, to the prison, and eventually the palace. Joseph probably questioned the process, but he never gave up on the promise. The Psalmist wrote this about Joseph:

> Then he sent someone to Egypt ahead of them—Joseph, who was sold as a slave. They bruised his feet with fetters and placed his neck in an iron collar. **Until the time came to fulfill his dreams, the Lord tested Joseph's character**. Then Pharaoh sent for him and set him free; the ruler of the nation opened his prison door. Joseph was put in charge of all the king's household; he became ruler over all the king's possessions.
>
> (Psalm 105:16-21, NLT)

What was meant for evil, turned for the good. The enemy devised a plan, but God prevailed. Though Joseph suffered, his character was being refined and tested by the Lord. God's process is about forming and preparing the person for the purpose. Joseph suffered for a season, but in the end, he ruled and reigned. Joseph rescued his people from a horrible famine as he fulfilled the vision for his life.

Hundreds of years later, a great prophet arose out of Egypt as a deliverer for Israel. Joseph brought his people into Egypt, saving them from a famine, and Moses led them out, rescuing his people from the oppression of slavery. Moses received his mandate from God while he was tending sheep on the backside of a desert. God grabbed the attention of this shepherd through a bush that burned but would not be consumed. It was a sign and wonder that Moses turned aside to observe. When Moses drew near, God's first words were, "Moses, Moses!" (Exodus 3:4). Moses responded, "Here I am" (Exodus 3:4). Little did Moses know, his life was about to change forever!

When God speaks your name, change is on the horizon. Moses got his name from Pharaoh's daughter, who found him in a basket that was floating on top of the water. He was born in Egypt under bondage. His mother was from the tribe of Levi and was one of the descendants who came to Egypt under Joseph's rule. When the Israelites prospered and multiplied in Egypt, Pharaoh and his leaders were threatened by their growth and prosperity, and they feared a possible mutiny from the Israelites. Their answer to this dilemma was to oppress them through slavery. The more the Israelites prospered, the heavier the demands and burdens Pharaoh and all of Egypt placed upon the people. Another answer was to send an edict out amongst the Israelites—any male, two years or younger, was ordered to be killed.

A young Jewish woman gave birth to a baby boy. Her faith in God inspired her to waterproof a basket and place her baby in it, sending him down the river in faith that he would be rescued and spared from death. Her faith was recorded thousands of years later in chapter eleven of the book of Hebrews. Pharaoh's daughter found the baby and drew him out of the water, and thus his name became Moses. Moses means: taken out or drawn.[1] When Pharaoh's daughter saw the basket amongst the reeds in the Nile River, she had her assistant retrieve the basket and, "When she opened it, she saw the child, and behold, the little boy was crying. So she had compassion on him and said, 'This is one of the Hebrew children'" (Exodus 2:6, Berean Study Bible). God's plan for deliverance was in motion.

For forty years, Moses lived in Egypt, but Egypt did not live within him. "By faith Moses, when he had grown up, refused to be known as the son of Pharaoh's daughter. He chose to be mistreated along with the people of God rather than to enjoy the fleeting pleasures of sin" (Hebrews 11:24-25, NIV). Moses attempted to be his people's deliverer before the appointed time. His disgust toward the constant abuse of slavery drove him to murder an Egyptian man who was inflicting pain on the Hebrew people. Though he attempted to cover up the act of murder, word began to spread and Moses fled from Egypt, fearing for his own life.

After forty years as a shepherd, God called his name, "Moses! Moses!" Do you remember what his name means? To be taken out or drawn out. God was drawing Moses out of the desert to his next assignment—Egypt. God heard the cries of his people, and Moses was the chosen one to deliver them from their horrible oppression. Their cries became his call. It was God's plan to anoint Moses as the deliverer for His people. When we think all hope is gone, God is in the mysterious places preparing His people to become the answer for the dilemma. When we think all is lost, God is orchestrating every move with our legacy in mind.

Esther became the Queen in a foreign land because God had the legacy and posterity of His people in mind. When wicked Haman had convinced the king to annihilate the Jews, Esther came into leadership "for such a time as this" (Esther 4:14). She refused to remain silent when her people needed a voice that would bring deliverance. Esther risked her life to leave a legacy of hope. Who knows what would've happened had she remained silent? Fear attempts to silence the plans and purposes of God. If we're going to leave a legacy of faith, we must go beyond our fears and surrender our lives completely to God's perfect plan. We must surrender to the One who knows the beginning and the end.

Gary Vaynerchuk says, "Please think about your legacy because you are writing it every day." Today, you are leaving a legacy through the choices you make. Nehemiah's journey began with a question, and Heaven's answer became his mission. One man's choice to obey God becomes another man's blessing. Nehemiah obeyed God and all of Jerusalem was blessed because of it. Chapters 8-13 of Nehemiah describe the reformation that escalated throughout Jerusalem and the surrounding areas. Ezra would read the Law and they would listen and repent. Nehemiah's choice to listen, trust, and obey stirred up a revival amongst his people, who were disinterested and lethargic at best. He obeyed God and he fought for his people! Your sons and daughters need you to rise up and fight the "good fight of faith"! Aren't they worth it? What's at stake if you don't?

Action Steps

1. Try to remember three choices you have made thus far in your life and write down the negative or positive results from that choice.
2. Seize this moment! Meditate and dream with God a favorable future. Once you begin to see that favorable future, write it down in your journal.
3. What decisions will you make today to get closer to fulfilling your favorable future?
4. Meditate and Journal your thoughts on the following Scripture: "And if anyone longs to be wise, ask God for wisdom and he will give it! He won't see your lack of wisdom as an opportunity to scold you over your failures but he will overwhelm your failures with his generous grace" (James 1:5, TPT).

Notes

1. *Hitchcock's Bible Names Dictionary*, Blue Letter Bible, accessed November 20, 2019, www.blueletterbible.org, Strong's H4871.

CHAPTER 16

SACRIFICIAL LEADERSHIP

"Remember for my good, O my God, all that I have done for this people."

(Nehemiah 5:19)

"Great achievement is usually born of great sacrifice, and is never the result of selfishness."

(Napoleon Hill)

The first great Transcontinental Railroad was built with much sacrifice. Over one hundred and fifty years ago, thousands of people rallied together to connect Eastern United States with Western United States. The efforts were not that short of miraculous! After much debate and little progress amongst our Nation's leaders at the time, our sixteenth President of the United States, Abraham Lincoln, made significant strides to see this vision become a reality. In an article written for the celebration of the 150th year of this accomplishment, the Union Pacific Railroad wrote this on their website, Up.com, "On July 1, 1862, after decades of debate and disagreement on the matter, Lincoln brought the transcontinental railroad to life with a stroke of his pen." They also wrote, "Union Pacific is proud to celebrate the legacy of Abraham Lincoln—who set the transcontinental railroad in motion and brought our railroad to life." Lincoln was a pacesetter in our country, and through his sacrificial leadership, much progress was made.

The Transcontinental Railroad was a vision to connect the entire United States from East to West. Others had the dream, but President Abraham Lincoln put the vision to action. Once the project was approved, workers were hired to start and finish the work. The Transcontinental project began in two separate locations. From the east, it began in Omaha, Nebraska, and in the west, Sacramento, California. The work was extremely hard, and the days were long. Many people who started the work, quit because of the arduous toil. Due to lack of laborers, the Central Pacific Railroad began to hire Chinese immigrants. The Railroad company hired fifty, then fifty more, and by the end of the project in the west, 90 percent of the laborers were Chinese immigrants.[1]

Leland Stanford was a major contributor and motivator of the Transcontinental Railroad. At the time, Stanford was the President of Central Pacific Railroad and the Governor of California. He was also the founder of Stanford University. He was known as one of the "Big Four" who made provisions for the project to be completed. Stanford had the honors of driving the last spike into the railroad tie that completed the first Transcontinental Railroad. The spike was made of gold and became known as "The Golden Spike." Though Stanford received much credit for the completion of the project, the Chinese immigrants were the ones who sacrificed their lives for the completion of it. In Commemoration of the 150th year of the first Transcontinental Railroad, Alex Shashkevich quotes Chang, Professor in the Humanities, "Without the Chinese migrants, the Transcontinental Railroad would not have been possible. If it weren't for their work, Leland Stanford could have been at best a footnote in history, and Stanford University may not even exist."[2]

The LA Times printed an article by Gordon Chang, who wrote, "Progress came at great cost: Many Chinese laborers died along the Central Pacific route. The company kept no records of deaths. But soon after the line was completed, Chinese civic organizations retrieved an estimated 1,200 bodies along the route and sent them home to China for burial."[3] Ultimately, many people made sacrifices to complete the Transcontinental Railroad. From President Lincoln, to Leland Stanford, the Irish immigrants, and of course, the Chinese immigrants. The vision wouldn't have become a reality without sacrifice.

In the pages of Holy Writ, sacrifice is at the heart of the message. Without sacrifice, we wouldn't have the invitation to be the Children of God. Without sacrifice, we wouldn't have any hope of redemption. With sacrifice, we have the forgiveness of sins and the promise of living abundant lives (John 10:10). The central figure of the Bible is the Son of God, Jesus Christ. The Apostle Paul wrote:

> Think of yourselves the way Christ Jesus thought of himself. He had equal status with God but didn't think so much of himself that he had to cling to the advantages of that status no matter what. Not at all. When the time came, he set aside the privileges of deity and took on the status of a slave, became human! Having become human, he stayed human. It was an incredibly humbling process. He didn't claim special privileges. Instead, he lived a selfless, obedient life and then died a selfless, obedient death—and the worst kind of death at that—a crucifixion.
>
> (Philippians 2:5-8, The Message Bible)

When I think of Abraham Lincoln, I think of a leader who made the ultimate sacrifice for his Nation. As described on the Independentsentinel.com website, M. Dowling said, "People might not agree on Lincoln but the one thing that people cannot take away from Lincoln is that he gave up everything for something he believed in, something that was far greater than himself." Sacrificial leaders are willing to do whatever it takes to fulfill the vision. They're motivated by leaving a reputable legacy more than they're motivated by building a personal kingdom. Lincoln made the right but difficult choices that would ultimately be the deciding factor of his fate. We know him as the President who issued the Emancipation Proclamation to free slaves in our Country, and that truly was his greatest cause, but he was also the one who signed the bill to start and finish the Transcontinental Railroad. Keep that in mind when you think of all the sacrifices made along the way to see this vision of the railroad in action and completed.

I'll follow leaders who make sacrifices of themselves to see a vision fulfilled. It's difficult to commit to something when the leader isn't fully invested. The leaders I have admired and followed for the past thirty years have been servant leaders, sacrificial in their time, energy, and money. What leader would call the troops to war without leading the way in some capacity? As a visionary leader, you can't require those you lead to make sacrifices without you leading the way. That would be like calling your church to a corporate time of prayer and fasting, and you as the leader feasting on food all day. Dave Ramsey says, "The most important decision about your goals is not what you're willing to do to achieve them, but what you are willing to give up." Sacrifice will be necessary at some point in the process of your vision coming to fruition.

Nehemiah was a sacrificial leader. While he was the cupbearer in the king's palace, he sacrificed food and fasted and prayed until he got his breakthrough. He left the comforts of the palace to journey hundreds of miles to a land that was ravaged from years of neglect. The palace was comfortably constructed, and the walls of Jerusalem were broken down and demolished. Nehemiah's retirement program was being obedient to the call of God. He left the comforts to embrace the life of obedience and sacrifice. Once he was established in Jerusalem and became her Governor, he continued to lead sacrificially.

Nehemiah makes account for the sacrifices he made to see the vision fulfilled:

> Moreover, from the time that I was appointed to be their governor in the land of Judah, from the twentieth year to the thirty-second year of Artaxerxes the king, twelve years, neither I nor my brothers ate the food allowance of the governor. The former governors who were before me laid heavy burdens on the people and took from them for their daily ration forty shekels of silver. Even their servants lorded it over the people. But I did not do so, because of the fear of God. I also persevered in the work on this wall, and we acquired no land, and all my servants were gathered there for the work. Moreover, there were at my table 150 men, Jews and officials, besides those who came to us from the nations that were around us. Now what was prepared at my expense for each day was one

ox and six choice sheep and birds, and every ten days all kinds of wine in abundance. Yet for all this I did not demand the food allowance of the governor, because the service was too heavy on this people.

(Nehemiah 5:14-18)

Nehemiah made sacrifices for the greater good of the people of Jerusalem. Let's break this down together:

1. Nehemiah didn't eat the amount of food that was allotted to him as the Governor.
2. Other Governors before him laid heavy burdens on the people and lorded it over them.
3. He worked diligently alongside the other laborers. As the leader, he could've sat back and watched them do the work.
4. Nehemiah didn't acquire his own land. He refused to use his position for privilege.
5. Nehemiah fed 150 men at his own expense each day they worked. They worked 52 days. Let's do the math: 52 oxen, 312 sheep, 312 choice birds, and an abundance of wine on 5 different occasions.

Nehemiah sacrificed at his own expense for the fulfillment of the vision that was branded within him. When God brands your heart with a vision, sacrifice becomes a joy. Take notice of the generosity flowing from Nehemiah's heart, through his hands, and unto the people he's leading. Nehemiah demonstrates the heart of God. When we co-labor with our Father in Heaven to impact the people of this planet, His heart bursts with joy and He demonstrates that through His continual provision. David Livingstone said, "If a commission by an earthly king is considered an honor, how can a commission by a Heavenly King be considered a sacrifice?" How true?

God is pleased when we make sacrifices for the greater good. A healthy balance is sacrifice that works through love and obedience. Why did Nehemiah make significant sacrifices? He said it himself, "...because of the fear of God" (Nehemiah 5:15b). Nehemiah demonstrated his love for God through his reverence for God. The fear of the Lord is different than an emotional fear that involves torment and separation. The fear of the Lord is a deep and profound respect for God, His Word, and His ways. The fear of God causes one to become not only a hearer of God's Word, but a doer of His Word. Out of this respect and love for God flows a love and respect for His people.

Why did Nehemiah make sacrifices? He feared God and loved people. Nehemiah's love for the people was evident when he said, "Yet for all this I did not demand the food allowance of the governor, because the service was too heavy on this people" (Nehemiah 5:18). Nehemiah is demonstrating the heart of a Shepherd. Making sacrifices for the people you lead is part of being "The Leader." At times it may be painful, but in those times, Father God is near. Turn your pain into pleasure by embracing a Heavenly perspective. A Heavenly perspective of sacrifice is announced in Romans 12:1, "I appeal to you therefore, brothers, by the mercies of God, to present your bodies as a living sacrifice, holy and acceptable to God, which is your spiritual worship." Because God has been so merciful toward us by sending His Son, Jesus, to become a sacrifice for our sins, it's an act of worship when we surrender our lives completely to Him. Our sacrifices then become our worship unto Him.

John Maxwell says, "Attitude determines your altitude." In the summer of 2019, my altitude was in the clouds more than it was above them. Christi and I led a project to start and finish a remodeling plan for our new childcare center. The project was in our church building and it consisted of tearing out old carpet, demolishing old walls, building new walls, sheet rocking, painting, laying down new carpet, electrical work, on and on and on! The outdoor projects involved removing rocks (many of them) from the future playground, trimming trees and bushes, tearing out dead bushes, on and on and on! The load of leading a church and the significant involvement with the remodeling project was stretching me thin. My attitude was affecting my altitude. I was challenged to fight off a bad attitude that stemmed from disappointment and wrestling to forgive people. Anger became a byproduct, along with a skewed perspective.

Back in 1992, I went skiing with my sister and cousin in the mountains of Washington. We started on the smaller slopes and eventually graduated to the larger ones later in the day. It was an overcast day, with clouds filling the sky.

As we ascended up the mountain on the chairlift, we began to travel through the clouds. It was a spectacular experience. What lay ahead was more special. As we ascended closer to the top of the mountain, we rose above the clouds and there it was—the sun shining in all of its brilliance! I looked down and saw a blanket of clouds under my feet. Once we reached the top, I looked out and saw other mountain peaks several miles away. I was in awe of God's creation and that moment of riding above the clouds. I didn't rush to get down the mountain, I remained on top as the view was etched in my mind forever. Perspective is everything!

Now that we're on the other side of the mountain with the childcare center, my perspective has changed. My head is no longer stuck in the clouds and obstructing my Heavenly view. I praise God for the advances we've made! Could I have possessed a better perspective before we completed the remodeling project? Absolutely! Had I realized deep within my heart that the sacrifices we were making in 2019 were an act of worship unto God, my perspective would've been clearer and my attitude would've changed my altitude.

Erwin Lutzer said, "Those who give much without sacrifice are reckoned as having given little." To keep your vision in action, sacrifice will be inevitable, but profitable. Our High School football coach, Coach Heupel, always said, "No pain, no gain!" Making sacrifices to see the vision come alive is part of the process. The key is remembering why you're making the sacrifices. Your sacrifice is an act of worship unto God and a demonstration of love to the people you're called to impact for His Glory! Keep your eyes on the prize! Keep your gaze on the Son! The clouds are momentary, but the sun continually shines in your season of sacrifice!

Action Steps

1. In your own words, what is sacrificial leadership? What does it look like? What is the motivation of a sacrificial leader?
2. What are you willing to sacrifice to see the vision accomplished?
3. What are you not willing to sacrifice to see the vision accomplished?

4.   Meditate and Journal your thoughts on the following Scripture: "And don't forget to do good and to share with those in need. These are the sacrifices that please God" (Hebrews 13:16, NLT).

Notes

1.   Lesley Kennedy, "Building the Transcontinental Railroad: How 20,000 Chinese Immigrants Made It Happen," May 10, 2019, last modified April 30, 2020, https://www.history.com/news/transcontinental-railroad-chinese-immigrants.
2.   Alex Shashkevich, "Stanford project gives voice to Chinese workers who helped build the Transcontinental Railroad," *Stanford News, Stanford University*, April 9, 2019.
3.   Gordon Chang, "Op-Ed: Remember the Chinese immigrants who built America's first transcontinental railroad," *LA Times*, (May 10, 2019). https://www.latimes.com/opinion/op-ed/la-oe-chang-transcontinental-railroad-anniversary-chinese-workers-20190510-story.html.

CHAPTER 17

REMAIN FOCUSED

"I am doing a great work and I cannot come down. Why should the work stop while I leave it and come down to you?"

(Nehemiah 6:3b)

Stay focused, believe that you can achieve at the highest level, surround yourself with others who believe in you, and do not stray from your goal.

(Zach Ertz)

Vision is a powerful force. With it, we're able to see beyond the unfinished product. Without it, we easily throw in the proverbial towel and chase after whatever the wind blows our way. The great and wise King Solomon wrote, "Where there is no prophetic vision the people cast off restraint, but blessed is he who keeps the law" (Proverbs 29:19). Prophetic vision brings direction, hope for the future, and divine encouragement. Where there's no prophetic vision, people will grow weary and give up. Vision is powerful! With it, we remain diligent in our efforts for a better day. Without it, we become lethargic and undisciplined.

This is the era of marathons and half marathons. Many people have become passionate about running a marathon for various reasons. Whatever their vision may be for running one, the same is true for everyone who decides to complete one—they have to become diligent in their preparation for the marathon. Most people don't decide to run their first marathon one day, and go for it the next. That only happens when someone has already been running and preparing for months. The commitment has to match the course. The runner begins to restrain themselves from eating certain foods, believing negative thoughts, and wasting quality time. The runner must set goals and follow through with them daily to achieve their goal of starting and finishing the race.

Nehemiah had a prophetic vision from the Lord to restore the walls around Jerusalem! With this Heavenly vision burning within him, Nehemiah remained focused on the course set before him. Without a vision, you will run aimlessly throughout your life. Why discipline yourself when there are no goals set to accomplish the vision? Nehemiah kept the vision of his heart alive, and this propelled him to work diligently everyday until the vision of the broken-down walls and gates was completely restored.

Let's take a look at how Nehemiah remained focused when opposing forces were beckoning for his attention:

1. Nehemiah possessed Discernment. Throughout the Book of Nehemiah, we see his discernment on display often. Opposing forces continually attempted to stop him and his co-laborers from rebuilding the walls around Jerusalem. Some attempts were more subtle than others, therefore, possessing discernment saved Nehemiah a lot of time and energy. Opposition is often a sign you're going in the right direction. It also comes at strategic times—right before you take steps toward the vision, and near the end of its completion. We're no threat to the enemy of our souls when we simply sit around and talk about a vision. We become a threat when we begin to take action. The strength of the winds of adversity may be a sign of our assignment's significance.

Nehemiah's enemies were Sanballat, Tobiah, and Geshem. Let's call them, "The Big Three." Right before Nehemiah completed the full restoration of the wall, The Big Three rose up to oppose him. They sent a message to Nehemiah, "Come and let us meet together at Hakkephirim in the plain of Ono" (Nehemiah 6:2). Nehemiah wrote, "But they intended to do me harm" (Nehemiah 6:2). Geshem quickly realized Nehemiah wouldn't take the bait, so he sent letters of accusation to Nehemiah: "That you and the Jews intend to rebel; that is why you are building the wall. And according to these reports you wish to become their king" (Nehemiah 6:6). Nehemiah discerned their plan, "For they all wanted to frighten us, thinking, 'Their hands will drop from the work, and it will not be done'" (Nehemiah 6:9). When pressing forward toward the completion of a vision, discernment can free us from confusion and fear.

The Big Three were relentless in their attempts to stop Nehemiah from finishing the project. They developed a much more subtle and deceptive approach. They hired someone else to communicate to Nehemiah. "Now when I went into the house of Shemaiah the son of Elaiah, son of Mehetabel, who was confined to his home, he said, 'Let us meet together in the house of God, within the temple. Let us close the doors of the temple, for they are coming to kill you. They are coming to kill you by night'" (Nehemiah 6:10). First, The Big Three tried to get Nehemiah to reason with them. Then, they sent false accusations. Last but not least, they hurled threats of killing him, hoping to create an intense fear in his heart so he would quit.

When the battle is raging in your mind, and thoughts of giving up are looming over your soul, cry out for discernment. "Yes, if you cry out for discernment, and lift up your voice for understanding, if you seek her as silver, and search for her as for hidden treasures; then you will understand the fear of the Lord, and find the knowledge of God. For the Lord gives wisdom; from His mouth come knowledge and understanding" (Proverbs 2:3-6, NKJV). Discernment reveals the intentions of one's heart and/or the motives of our enemy, Satan. "The first step on the way to victory is to recognize the enemy" (Corrie Ten Boom). Discernment keeps me in peace and equips me for the battle. If I know the strategy of my enemy, I can pray more effectively. If I discern why this battle is raging against me, I will stand strong, knowing I'm about to receive my breakthrough.

Nehemiah was strengthened through understanding, "And I understood and saw that God had not sent him, but he had pronounced the prophecy against me because Tobiah and Sanballat had hired him. For this purpose he was hired, that I should be afraid and act in this way and sin, and so they could give me a bad name in order to taunt me" (Nehemiah 6:13). Charles Spurgeon once said, "Discernment is not a matter of simply telling the difference between right and wrong; rather it is telling the difference between right and almost right." Nehemiah's enemies tried to lure him into the Temple, into the holy place. Going into the Temple would seem to be a righteous endeavor, but Nehemiah knew it wasn't his place. The Priests were set apart by God to enter into the Temple. Nehemiah knew his place and humbly remained in his sphere of God-given authority. King Uzziah overstepped his God-given realm of authority and was smitten with leprosy (2 Chronicles 26:1). Nehemiah's discernment probably saved him an early death.

2. Nehemiah learned to delegate. John Maxwell says, "If you want to do a few small things right, do them yourself. If you want to do great things and make a big impact, learn to delegate." Nehemiah mastered the art of delegation. He was a servant leader who empowered everyone around him to work on the walls of Jerusalem. Nehemiah delegated jobs and remained focused on his responsibility as the leader of the massive project. He was a true servant leader.

When Nehemiah was petitioned five times to come down from the wall and converse with The Big Three (Sanballat, Tobiah, and Gershem), he responded by sending someone else to report back to his enemies, "And I sent messengers to them, saying, 'I am doing a great work and I cannot come down. Why should the work stop while I leave it and come down to you?'" (Nehemiah 6:3). Robert Half says, "Delegating work works, provided the one delegating works, too." Nehemiah did just that. He remained steadfast on finishing the wall through the power of delegation.

Jesus is our model for life and ministry. He is the Master Delegator. As our Chief Apostle (Hebrews 3:1), He was sent by God on a mission to this planet. His mission was:

1. To seek and save the lost (Luke 19:10).
2. To destroy the works of the devil (1 John 3:8).
3. To become a sacrifice for our sins (John 3:16-17; 1 John 2:2; Romans 5:8).
4. To give us an abundant life (John 10:10-11).

Knowing that He would become the ultimate and only true sacrifice for our sins, rise from the dead, and then ascend to the right hand of the Father, He modeled life and ministry to His twelve disciples. A disciple is a student, a pupil, one who learns from another.[1] The disciples learned from Jesus and became His sent ones and messengers throughout the known world of their time. Jesus was a disciple-maker who empowered His disciples to do the same, "Go therefore and make disciples of all nations, baptizing them in the name of the Father and of the Son and of the Holy Spirit" (Matthew 28:19). The art of delegating isn't merely getting someone to do something for you, but to empower and equip others to fulfill their mission on this planet.

Nehemiah modeled leadership through his focus, determination, and his ability to get the job done. He knew the vision would never be accomplished through himself alone. From start to finish, he gathered people and gave them the authority to accomplish the task. Have you ever been given an assignment from a boss, but not the authority to make any decisions or the power to determine your course of action to complete the project? No one likes to be micromanaged. Progress is severely impeded when you have someone looking over your shoulder at all times. Completing the reconstruction of the walls around Jerusalem would have taken fifty-two years rather than fifty-two days if Nehemiah had taken that approach.

Nehemiah learned to say "no" so he could say "yes." If we say "yes" to everything, we will say "no" to the most important things. As a pastor, I receive many requests for my time, energy, and attention. I have learned to guard myself from becoming too busy with matters that restrict me from fulfilling my God-given vision. When I was younger, I disliked the word "balance," mostly because of the context it was used in. Balance is a great word. Each week, I keep a schedule that is much more balanced. I protect my Thursday nights. Every Thursday night is my date night with my wife. I protect my Friday nights. Every Friday night is our family night. Not only do I have a vision to plant multiple churches, write books, and preach in other Nations, I have a vision for a healthy marriage and family. Not everyone appreciates it when I say "no," but that's okay. You must learn to say "no" so you can say "yes." Plus, it's imperative that you know it's okay to say it. Embrace it! Love it! Live it! Once you do, you're closer to fulfilling the vision for your life.

3. Nehemiah Prayed. Roy T. Bennet said, "What you stay focused on will grow." Staying focused on God increases our awareness of Him and the fact that He's always near. Throughout Nehemiah's journey as a cupbearer, then the leader of a massive project, he had conversations with God. He prayed!

Prayer is essential while you're taking action steps toward fulfilling the vision. Martin Luther said, "To be a Christian without prayer is no more possible than to be alive without breathing." Corrie Ten Boom asked a great question, "Is prayer your steering wheel or your spare tire?" Nehemiah demonstrated a life of action. His action was fueled by his prayer life. His relationship with God empowered him to start and finish strong. In the last two days of working on the wall, Nehemiah had intense opposition. He went to his source of strength, "Remember Tobiah and Sanballat, O my God, according to these things that they did, and also the prophetess Noadiah and the rest of the prophets who wanted to make me afraid" (Nehemiah 6:14). Nehemiah was looking to God for his strength. He knew God had empowered him to restore the wall, and it was ultimately God's responsibility to do whatever He wanted with his enemies. He hurled this burden upon the Lord.

I want to propose to you that Nehemiah possessed discernment, determination, and the ability to delegate through his relationship with God. Jesus told His disciples, "Apart from me you can do nothing" (John 15:5b). The sooner we discover this truth, the sooner we'll begin to soar in this life. How much energy and time have we wasted through our futile attempts to complete the vision in our own strength? Your prayer life is your lifeline! "We can do nothing without prayer. All things can be done by importunate prayer" (E. M. Bounds). One of my all-time favorite verses is from the book of Jeremiah, "Call to Me, and I will answer you, and show you great and mighty things, which you do not know" (Jeremiah 33:3). God's promise is to answer us and show us great and mighty things!

Our church just completed a twenty-one day fast. The first seven days were brutal for me. I was cold and tired the whole week. My theme for the fast was, "Coming into Alignment for His Assignment." I was believing God for direction, wisdom, financial miracles, and transformation. On the fifth day of our fast, God spoke to Christi and I at separate times during the day. We both heard the same thing in different ways. Christi felt God was saying, "You will not hire a Family Life Pastor this year. You and Drew must become established in your different roles at Freedom Church." I didn't hear that, but later that night at the corporate prayer meeting, I began to pray about hiring a new pastor. While I was praying, I didn't have peace about hiring someone new. I felt like we needed to wait. Two days later, Christi and I began to discuss what we both felt. I was amazed and relieved. God is good! If we talk to Him and then listen, He will save us from making decisions we would later regret.

Through Nehemiah's relationship with God, he remained focused throughout the process of completing the vision. Discernment and delegation became his friends while his enemies were viciously attempting to halt the work God was accomplishing through him. Embrace God, cry out for discernment, and be determined to say "no" so you can say "yes." This is your time! This is your hour! You will remain focused and you will finish the race that has been set before you! What started with a question mark is about to turn into a big exclamation point! It's time to finish!

Action Steps

1. Are you saying "Yes" to tasks that you should be saying "No" to? If so, what?
2. Make a plan to delegate tasks and projects that consume too much of your time. Make a list of those tasks, then write down an action plan to equip someone else to complete the tasks.
3. Commit to praying over your day and asking God for discernment.
4. Meditate and Journal your thoughts on the following Scripture: "And it is my prayer that your love may abound more and more, with knowledge and all discernment, so that you may approve what is excellent, and so be pure and blameless for the day of Christ" (Philippians 1:9-10).

Notes

5. Strong's 3100.

CHAPTER 18

IT IS FINISHED!

"So the wall was finished on the twenty-fifth day of the month Elul, in fifty-two days."

(Nehemiah 6:15)

"Stopping at third adds no more to the score than striking out. It doesn't matter how well you start if you fail to finish."

(Billy Sunday)

What started with a question ended with an exclamation! God is gracious enough to bless us with the desire and anoint us with the ability. He will do his part, and we must be disciplined enough to work with Him to finish the task. Nehemiah had obstacles, but he learned to overcome them and make them his fuel to finish. When the excitement of starting something new is now in your rearview mirror, it's best to gaze through the windshield in front of you until you arrive at your destination. The thrill of starting something new isn't the final destination, it's only the beginning. The glory comes when you finish.

Jesus was praying when He said, "I have glorified You on the earth. I have finished the work which You have given Me to do" (John 17:4). How did Jesus give glory to His Father in Heaven? He finished the work that was given to Him by Father God. Jesus fulfilled the vision. How could He say this before the Cross? I believe He declared this, knowing He had done everything He saw his Father doing up until that moment (Read John 5:19). Jesus knew the

Cross was before him, and he was committed to running to the finish line so He could boldly and confidently say, "IT IS FINISHED!" (John 19:30). The ultimate goal of keeping your vision in action is to finish what has been started.

What's at stake if you don't finish? If Nehemiah had quit, Jerusalem would have remained vulnerable to attacks from their enemies. Nehemiah's obedience unto the Heavenly vision was not just about him, but the masses of people he would impact in a powerful way. Bobby Conner says, "Revolutions begin with the few and then spread to the masses." After the wall was completed in fifty-two days, the Jewish people began to seek God in a way they hadn't for years. Revival started with Nehemiah, then spread like a prairie fire amongst God's People.

The people turned to God as Ezra the Priest read the Law to them. They began to hear and understand what God desired of them. Before Nehemiah was obedient to God, he wasn't given a guarantee from God that the people would follow him and turn their hearts towards Heaven. Nehemiah obeyed God each step of the way, then the fruit of his obedience came. These people were once hardened and rebellious toward God, but after the completion of the wall, they became soft and repentant. After they heard the reading of God's Word, they began to weep and confess their sins. A revolution that started in Nehemiah's heart spread to the masses. Your decision to follow God affects people unbeknownst to you now. Don't let what you can't see influence your decision to obey God. A good friend of mine, Dean Niforatos, says, "Delayed obedience is disobedience." Let's be quick to hear and respond with a "YES" to God's vision for our lives!

You don't know who you will impact through your obedience to God. I'm reminded of a cold winter night in 1993 when I was living in Baltimore, MD. I was a young Youth Pastor who knew very little about pastoring, but just enough to be able to respond to God's nudging. After our youth service on a Wednesday night, I felt led to visit a young man I'd never met. I heard about him through some of our youth at the church, but never had the opportunity to meet him myself. But on that cold night in January, I asked one of our youth kids to drive me to this young man's house. When we got there, I felt a boldness on me. I rang the doorbell. Someone answered the door and I asked if Kenny (not his real name) was there. They let me in and I met Kenny for the first time. Things looked a little shady, if you know what I mean. I sensed some shenanigans going on and also felt a depressing spirit in the atmosphere.

I asked Kenny to come out to my car with me. Get the picture here, I was sitting in my car with a complete stranger, asking serious questions. I had no relational equity with this young man, only a strong leading from the Lord. One of the last questions I asked was, "Have you been suicidal?" Kenny responded with a yes. Then I asked him, "Can I pray for you?" He responded with another yes. I can't remember what I said or asked for in my prayer, but I do remember literally crying out to God with a loud voice of desperation for this young man. The next thing I know, the Presence of God filled that car and Kenny was crying like a baby! The power of God touched that young man and he was blessed from head to toe.

After Kenny started sobbing, he told me he was planning to kill himself that night. God knew his pain and heard his cry for help. His cry became my call! When I was depressed and suicidal in 1991, I never knew I would be in Baltimore, MD, two years later, rescuing a young man from destruction. The vision that God has placed in your heart is real! Don't quit! Don't give in to the lies that your life doesn't matter and you aren't making a difference. Your obedience to the Heavenly vision will make an impact!

In every stage of life, we're starting and finishing. Each grade we start, we finish. I started grade school at O.M. Tiffany and I finished after my 6th grade. I began middle school at Holgate and finished after my 9th grade year. I began my 10th grade at Aberdeen Central and then graduated after my Senior year. Every stage was preparation for the next. I began my freshman year of college at Moorhead State University in Minnesota and finished five years later. Each step is an important step. We glorify our greater accomplishments, but without every step of starting and then finishing, we aren't prepared for the next stage of life. It's important to finish strong in whatever season you may be in.

For twelve months, starting June of 1993 and then ending after May of 1994, I was an intern pastor at First Assembly of God (now Northview Church) in Fargo, ND. I began this journey with much excitement and anticipation. The pastors and people were spectacular! I was honored to be a part of something that was alive and moving. Making $25.00 monthly was not a problem for me because I loved the opportunity to learn under the tutelage of pastors who I highly respected.

Toward the end of my internship in 1994, I began to question the value of my time spent as an intern. I began to ask, "Why was I here this past year? What did it accomplish?" I was called to preach but didn't have many opportunities to do that. Most of that year, I served in many different capacities that I never felt called to. At the time, I thought, "What is the value of this?" I drove the bus Tuesday nights, Wednesday nights, Thursday nights, Friday nights, Saturday mornings, and sometimes Sunday mornings. I thought, "I'm just a glorified bus driver." Now I didn't just drive a bus, since every time I drove, it was for a specific ministry I was involved in. But it felt like I was just spinning my wheels at times. When we're in a process, our present season can become cloudy because we're unaware of the good work God is accomplishing in us.

It was the last week of my internship and I was preparing to preach to the Youth of First Assembly. The large sanctuary at First Assembly was an inviting place to pray and prepare for the message I was about to preach. I accessed the thirty-five hundred seat auditorium from the balcony and descended to the altar from the staircase. The lights were off and there was very little lighting from a few small windows as I walked down the steps. I remember thinking, "Why was I here this year?" I stepped on the last step, at least what I thought was the last step, and almost fell over when I missed it. Did that make sense? After I stood up straight and caught my breath from the shock of missing the last step, I heard this in my spirit, "That's why you were here!" God began to speak to my heart.

In a matter of a few minutes, I was comforted and encouraged by God as to why I interned in Fargo, North Dakota. In that moment I realized this was an important step in the development of my character. We like to take shortcuts in our development. Sometimes we think we're ready for our next assignment and then step out of God's timing before we complete the season we're in. Had I quit the internship, I would've aborted God's plan of development for my life. We miss valuable steps of formation when we quit in the middle of the process. Had Nehemiah quit during the painful process of completing the wall, he would have never led his people to a time of restoration and reformation. Finishing strong in one season prepares us for the next.

After my internship in Fargo, I became a Youth Pastor in Beulah. I began to use the tools I was equipped with in Fargo for my time in Beulah. This was a time of discovery for me. Mark Elhardt says, "Preparation time is never wasted time." John Tasch says, "It's better to prepare the way than repair the way." One completed season leads to the next. Not only are we prepared for the next season, we become more confident in that season. Our confidence is built on the fact that we finished something we may have never thought was possible. When we complete an assignment given to us by God, He will promote us to the next season. We begin to build a history with God, and that builds confidence. It's important for us to remind ourselves of what we have come through. We can glance back at our past victories with God and rejoice that He is faithful. If He was faithful in our past season, we can be confident He'll be faithful in the next season.

Joyce Meyer says, "Getting organized in the normal routines of life and finishing little projects you've started is an important first step toward realizing larger goals. If you can't get a handle on the small things, how will you ever get it together to focus on the big things?" What may appear to be a small victory is, in reality, a huge victory. Each accomplished task or vision builds us up for the next. If we're faithful in the small things, God will trust us with larger things. Jesus said, "The one who manages the little he has been given with faithfulness and integrity will be promoted and trusted with greater responsibilities. But those who cheat with the little they have been given will not be considered trustworthy to receive more" (John 16:10, TPT). Maybe your next season of fruitfulness and impact has not emerged because you haven't been faithful in your present season?

At fifty, I'm much more aware of the value of finishing what I have started. Had I skipped the internship, there would have been no Beulah. Had there been no Beulah, I would have missed the opportunity of a lifetime—meeting Christi and marrying my best friend and the love of my life. No Christi, no Nehemiah, Ezekiel, Faith, and Mercy (my children). Beulah was not only the starting place for my family, but a training place for life and ministry. During my first few months in Beulah, I was convinced my stay there would be three years. God's plan was much different. I lived in Beulah for almost nine years. I finished the race that was set before me in Beulah. My time in Beulah prepared me for traveling and preaching full time and starting Freedom Church in Aberdeen. My full-time travels prepared me to become a better preacher. If we're faithful and patient in one season, God will promote us to the next season. The prophet Zechariah said, "Do not despise these small beginnings, for the Lord rejoices to see the work begin" (Zechariah 4:10a, NLT). Surrender your season to the Lord and watch Him prepare you for a bright future.

The Apostle Paul wrote to his spiritual son, "As for me, my life has already been poured out as an offering to God. The time of my death is near. I have fought the good fight, I have finished the race, and I have remained faithful. And now the prize awaits me—the crown of righteousness, which the Lord, the righteous Judge, will give me on the day of his return. And the prize is not just for me but for all who eagerly look forward to his appearing" (2 Timothy 4:6-8, NLT). Paul finished strong. Paul poured out everything he had within for the sake of the Gospel. He became a living epistle, a living sacrifice unto God. Knowing his time of departure was near, he wanted his spiritual son to know he "fought the good fight, finished the race, and remained faithful." Is there a better testimony? May this be our testimony!

Finishing strong requires us to fight for the sake of advancing God's vision for our lives and remaining faithful throughout the process. Paul gives a key to accomplishing this, "And now the prize awaits me—the crown of righteousness" (2 Timothy 4:8a). Looking forward to the Heavenly reward will keep us on the path of righteousness. Looking forward to God's applause rather than the praise of people empowers us to finish the race that has been set before us. Vision in Action is about receiving our instructions from God's Word, understanding our unique purpose on this planet, and running the race that has been set before us by God. He created us and fashioned us for His purpose. When we surrender to His vision, we will receive His rewards. Are you longing to see Him and hear, "Job well done"?

Connie Campbell Bratcher wrote a beautiful poem on Faithpoetry.com:

Oh, to hear those words when we see His face,
At the end of time in that glorious place.
We'll bow before Him, worshipping our King,
As we hear the host of angels sing.
A crown of righteousness awaits we're told,
For our faithfulness within the fold;
But at His feet our crown we'll cast,
When our wonderful Saviour we meet at last.
Yes, face to face we'll see Him there,
The one who died, our sins to bear.
He made the way for our spiritual birth,
And abundant life upon the earth.
As we enter into glory with our merciful King,
Along with the angels we'll eternally sing...
Praises to His name for His marvelous grace,
Enabling us to enter His Holy Place –
And as faithful servants who've received God's Son,
We'll hear His voice say to us..."Well Done."

His Lord said unto him, well done
thou good and faithful servant.

(Matt. 25:21)

Action Steps

1. Who will be impacted the most if you don't follow through with the vision God has given you?
2. Ask God to give you a picture of His desire and dreams for your life. Write it down in your journal and commit to meditating on it weekly.
3. What is your plan to finish strong? Make a plan, write it down, and set goals and action plans.
4. Meditate and Journal your thoughts on the following Scripture: "Therefore, since we are surrounded by so great a cloud of witnesses, let us also lay aside every weight, and sin which clings so closely, and let us run with endurance the race that is set before us" (Hebrews 12:1).

BIBLIOGRAPHY

Bennett, Roy T. *The Light in the Heart*. Roy T. Bennett, 2020.

Bergen, Peter L. "September 11 Attacks." *Encyclopedia Britannica*, 2001.

Bush, George W. "Text of Bush's Address." Cable News Network, 2001.

Chang, Gordon. "Op-Ed: Remember the Chinese immigrants who built America's first transcontinental railroad." *LA Times*, (May 10, 2019). https://www.latimes.com/opinion/op-ed/la-oe-chang-transcontinental-railroad-anniversary-chinese-workers-20190510-story.html.

Encyclopaedia Judaica. Jerusalem: Encyclopaedia Judaica, 1996.

Frangipane, Francis. *The Three Battlegrounds*. Cedar Rapids, IA: Arrow Publications, 2006.

Graham, Billy. *Hope for Each Day: Words of Wisdom and Faith*. Nashville, TN: Thomas Nelson, 2017.

HELPS Word – Studies. Bible Hub: Search, Read, Study the Bible in Many Languages. Copyright © 1987, 2011 by Helps Ministries, Inc. Accessed November 15, 2019. www.biblehub.com.

Hitchcock's Bible Names Dictionary. Blue Letter Bible. Accessed November 20, 2019. www.blueletterbible.org.

Jacey Fortin contributed reporting. A version of this article appears in print on July 4, 2019, Section B, Page 16 of the New York edition with the headline: "Lee Iacocca, Who Got Ford and Chrysler Humming, Is Dead at 94."

Kelly, James. "To Our Readers." *Time Magazine*, September 11, 2001.

Kennedy, Lesley. "Building the Transcontinental Railroad: How 20,000 Chinese Immigrants Made It Happen." May 10, 2019. Last modified April 30, 2020. https://www.history.com/news/transcontinental-railroad-chinese-immigrants.

Kidner, Derek and Donald J. Wiseman. *The Tyndale Old Testament commentaries. An Introduction and Commentary on Books I and II of the Psalms.* Leicester: Inter-Varsity Press, 1979.

Kidner, Derek. *Ezra And Nehemiah: An Introduction and Commentary.* Tyndale Old Testament Commentaries, Volume 12. General Editor: Donald J. Wiseman. Downers Grove, IL: IVP Academic, 2009.

Meah, Asad. "35 Inspirational Lee Iacocca Quotes On Success." *Awaken the Greatness Within*, (May 19, 2018). https://www.awakenthegreatnesswithin.com/35-inspirational-lee-iacocca-quotes-on-success/.

Meyer, Joyce. *Battlefield of the mind: Winning the Battle in Your Mind.* New York: FaithWords, 2017.

Mullen, David and Phil Vischer. "Jonah Was a Prophet." *Jonah: A VeggieTales Movie.* Who'S Jo, Who'S Jo Music, 2002, compact disc.

Munroe, Myles. *Understanding Your Potential: Discovering the Hidden You.* Shippensburg: Destiny Image, Inc., 2011.

Shashkevich, Alex. "Stanford project gives voice to Chinese workers who helped build the Transcontinental Railroad." *Stanford News, Stanford University*, April 9, 2019.

Smith, Michael W., Amy Grant and Wayne Kirkpatrick. "Place In This World," 1990, track 3 on *Go West Young Man*, Reunion, 1991, compact disc.

Strong's Hebrew Lexicon (KJV). Blue Letter Bible. Accessed November 7, 2019. www.blueletterbible.org.

Thayer's Greek Lexicon Electronic Database. Blue Letter Bible. Copyright © 2002, 2003, 2006, 2011 by Biblesoft, Inc. Accessed November 5, 2019. www.blueletterbible.org.

The Merriam-Webster Dictionary. Springfield, MA: Merriam-Webster, 2019.

Made in the USA
Columbia, SC
26 August 2020